...g
...
...f

...ead of crucian carp. There are
also a few large carp, well into
double figures.The high quality
roach and perch also makes this
water one of the best winter
fishing venues in the area.

WIRE MILL DAM
FISHERY

Ringinglow Road

Whiteley Wood Lane

Knowle Lane

Bents Road

Ecclesall Road

Fish-it 2

Published by:
Arc Publishing and Print
166 Knowle Lane
Sheffield S11 9SJ

Produced By: Chris Keeling

ISBN: 978-0-9555911-0-5

ACKNOWLEDGMENTS

I would like to thank the following for there
help in producing this guide:
Gary Mackender for art direction and cover design.
Billy Clarke Fishing Tackle for information useful in
researching venues.
South Yorkshire Tourism for the use of their map.
Doncaster & District Angling Association.
Denaby Miners Welfare A.C.
Clive Nuttall secretary of Catcliffe, Treeton Anglers Alliance.
All fishery owners and angling clubs who have kindly
provided information.

Arc Publishing and Print
166 Knowle Lane
Sheffield
S11 9SJ

C O N T E N T S

ACKNOWLEDGMENTS 2

CONTENTS 3

WELCOME...4

ABOUT THIS GUIDE 5

SOUTH YORKSHIRE MAP 6

SPECIES / SYMBOLS 7

KNOTS...8

SECTION 1 9

SECTION 2 43

SECTION 3 63

RIVERS 83

FISHING TACKLE SHOPS............................91

INDEX 92

VOUCHERS 93

W E L C O M E

Welcome to the 2nd edition of **Fish-it South Yorkshire.**
The success of the first guide has forced me to bring
out this new updated version with new information, new
venues and a new section on rivers. To encourage an
angler to try a new fishery, many owners have
generously agreed to a discounted price on your first
visit. So take this guide with you when you go fishing
and give a different venue a try. You will find your
discount vouchers at the back of the guide.
During the last two years I have found many new ponds
to fish and have included them in this guide. Have a
look at the rivers section and discover the delights of
river fishing as I recently did.
Hopefully you will find this updated version of Fish-it
South Yorkshire a useful guide to trying different places
to fish.

Chris Keeling

A B O U T   T H I S   G U I D E

To help you locate a fishery, this book has been split into three sections each covering different areas of South Yorkshire and the surrounding area.

Section A — South and West of Barnsley, Rotherham and Sheffield.

Section B — North of Barnsley across to the North of Doncaster.

Section C — South and East of Doncaster, and south towards Worksop.

Rivers — Rivers in and around South Yorkshire

Each page contains details of a fishery, with information on the following:

Ticket Price: All day ticket costs plus details on OAPs, disabled and junior concessions

Directions: Usually from the nearest city or town, or from the closest motorway junction.

Description: A brief outline of what the fishery looks like plus details on features such as islands, depths and the best places to fish.

Types of Fish: List of species present, many with estimated weights.

Rules/Bans: The restrictions set by the fishery on type of baits, hooks etc.

Number of Lakes: The number of waters available to fish at the venue.

Facilities: What is available at each location i.e. cafe.

Telephone: The number of the owner, angling club secretary or match organiser.

SOUTH YORKSHIRE

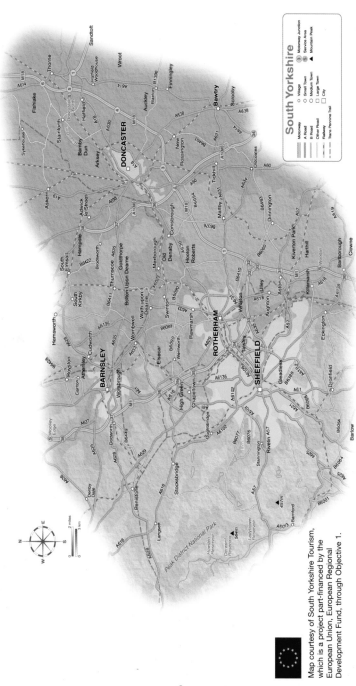

Map courtesy of South Yorkshire Tourism, which is a project part-financed by the European Union, European Regional Development Fund, through Objective 1.

S P E C I E S / S Y M B O L S

Most commonly found in
the South Yorkshire area.

 BARBEL

 Camping

 BREAM

 Caravan Site

 CARP

 Drinks

 CHUB

 Disabled Access

 CRUCIAN

 Toilets

 IDE

 Food

 ORFE

 Parking

 PERCH

 DACE

 PIKE

 GUDGEON

 ROACH

 Location of fishery on Section Maps

 RUDD

To help you find the nearest place to get tackle and bait, you will find a list of fishing tackle shops in South Yorkshire on page 91

 TENCH

TROUT

7

Blood Knot

This knot can be used to join two lines together, start by overlapping the ends of the two lines.

Thread the end of your line through the eye of your hook.

Twist one end round the other line four times and pass it between the two lines.

Pass the free underneath the line and bring it back over the line to form a loop

Do the same with the other end of line, making sure the previous step does not come undone.

Before pulling tight wet the knot to lubricate this also make it hold better. Trim off the two ends.

Pull on the loose end to tighten. Trim the line.

Half Blood Knot

Used mainly for joining hook to line.

Continue to loop the free over the line about four times.

Pass the loose end between the eye of the hook and the first loop.

Double Overhand loop

This knot is used to create a loop at the end of a line. Also known as the surgeon's loop.

To begin, double the end of the line back against itself.

Tie an overhand knot in the doubled line.

The doubled end should then be tucked through the loop again.

Pull the knot as tight as possible and trim of the end.

Water Knot

This knot can also be known as the surgeon's knot. It is useful for joining a lighter hook line to your mainline

Hold the ends of the two lines alongside each other so that they overlap by about six inches.

Take hold of the two lines and make a wide loop.

Holding the two lines together. Pass the ends of the line through the loop four times.

Pull the lines tightly so that the loop makes a knot. Trim the two ends.

S Woolley Edge
38
A636
Carlton
A637
Denby Dale
A635
BARNSLEY
A628
Dodworth
37
Worsbrough
4
3
A61
M1
Penistone
B6449
A633
A629
5
land
Elsecar
10
6
A616
7
8
B6090
9
A616
Stocksbridge
High Green
Wentworth
41
Chapeltown
35
Rawmarsh
A629
Oughtibridge
13
ROTHERHAM
A6102
A6135
11
14
A6102
34
12
17
B6077
32
Whiston
B6076
A6109
34
A57
A6101
Tinsley
33
Stannington
19
23
SHEFFIELD
A630
Rivelin A57
Aughton
▲ 457m
15
Gleadless
16/33
20
21
B6388
Aston
31
ford
A621
22
A57
A6102
24
M1
B6068
26
27
28
25
18
Killamarsh
B6001
A625
Eckington
A618
A625
B6054
Dronfield
A6135
30
B6054
29
Barlow

≡≡≡ Motorway	○ Village	③ Motorway Junction
━━ A Road	○ Small Town	Ⓢ Service Area
━━ B Road	◎ Medium Town	▲ Mountain Peak
── Other Road	□ Large Town	
┄┄ Railway	☐ City	
┄ Trans Pennine Trail		

Abbeydale Dam

Abbeydale Industrial Hamlet, Sheffield.

1/2 PRICE VOUCHER AT BACK OF BOOK

Ticket Price: Day ticket £5.00 (£4.00 after 4pm) Available from Woodseats Angling Shop.

Directions: From the centre of Sheffield take the A621 (Abbeydale Road). After about 3 miles go straight on at the traffic lights at Beauchief. The Dam is 300 yards on your left just after the Hamlet entrance.

Description: This well run water is between 4 and 5 acres in size. The depth varies from the dam wall end at around 20 feet to a foot deep at the far end. The 10 day ticket pegs which are next to the road are an ideal depth of between 5 and 6 feet. Fishing is very good from any of these pegs with the dominant species being rudd and tench. This is not a carp lake so don't expect to be snapped by a twenty pounder. The bank next to the railway line is for season permit holders only, contact the bailiff for details.

Types of Fish: Bream, tench, roach, rudd and crucian carp.

Rules/Bans: Barbless hooks, no groundbait, no meats, no boilies, no night fishing.

Number of Lakes: One

Facilities: None

 15

Telephone: 0114 2589578 or 0779 2657669

Aston Ponds.

Aston Ponds, Aston, Sheffield.

Ticket Price: Day tickets are £5.00, Concessions at £4.00.

Directions: From junction 31 of the M1, take the A57 towards Sheffield, at the roundabout turn left heading towards Killamarsh. Turn left after a few metres and follow the lane to the ponds.

Description: Most of the pegs at this large five pond fishery are suitable for anglers with disabilities. The waters have plenty of bankside features to target. You are spoiled for choice with so many good pegs to chose from, but you can't go wrong fishing for carp with some luncheon meat on the Split Pond next to the road ..

Types of Fish: This water has large stocks of silver fish, with roach and perch to a good size. Stable Pond has been stocked heavily with carp. Bream and chub feature to 5lb with roach and perch to just over 2lb. There are some very big carp to over 30lb, but the main stock of carp are less than 5lb in weight.
More carp and ide have been re-stocked recently.

Rules/Bans: Keepnets only in matches. Barbless hooks only. Ground bait by feeder or pole cup only.

Number of Lakes: Five

Facilities:

 16

Telephone: 0114 2653541 or 07771 851185

Barlow Fishery

Barlow Trout and Coarse Fishery, Barlow.

FREE FISHING VOUCHER AT BACK OF BOOK

Ticket Price: Day ticket £4.00 After 1pm £3.00 Juniors, OAP's £3.00. Matches by arrangement.
Trout Lakes: Full day £14.00 four fish taken. Six Hours £12.00 three fish taken. Six Hours £10.00 two fish taken. £7.00 sport ticket ring for details.

Directions: The fishery is located in the village of Barlow on the B6051, midway between Chesterfield and Owler Bar. Look out for the signs at the west end of the village.

Description: A great fishery for all ages and abilities with the last of the four lakes (pictured) being most suitable for beginners. This well established fishery gives the angler plenty of choice with four coarse lakes and four trout lakes, plus a small brook. The four coarse lakes are stocked with a variety of fish with the largest carp being in the first two waters. The third pond is the tench pond and the last one is mixed. The cafe serves a great bacon sandwich.

Types of Fish: Carp, rudd, bream, tench, roach, trout, barbel, and chub.

Rules/Bans: Barbless hooks only, no keepnets, no hard baits, no ground bait, no hemp.

Number of Lakes: Four coarse, four trout.

Facilities:

 29

Telephone: 0114 2890543

Bradleys Ponds
Geer Lane, Ford, Sheffield.

Ticket Price: Day ticket £5.00. £3.00 after 4pm

Directions: From the A6102 Sheffield ring road at Gleadless turn onto White Lane signposted Mosborough. After a mile turn right to Ridgeway. Follow the road till you reach Ford. Turn left after the pub on the corner and continue up Geer Lane untill you reach the farm. The ponds are on your left.

Description: There are three ponds to try. I prefer the middle one which is also the largest at around two acres.
This pond has a small island at one end which I fished up to using a 13 metre pole. I caught a few carp at an average weight of 8lb + plenty of silver fish. This is a popular fishery set in an attractive valley of a working farm.

Types of Fish: Carp, bream, tench, perch, roach and rudd.

Rules/Bans: No carp in keepnets, No cereal ground baits except bread punch, barbless hooks only. No dogs. No night fishing.

Number of Lakes: Three

Facilities: P

Telephone: 01246 435563

Carterhall Fishery

Charnock Hall, Sheffield.

1/2 PRICE VOUCHER AT BACK OF BOOK

Ticket Price: Day ticket £4.00   Concessions £3.00

Directions: Turn off the A6102, Sheffield ring road and head towards Ridgeway on the B6388. Take the third right turn into Carterhall Road. Turn left just after the school and follow the lane down to the farm. Look for the fishing sign.

Description: Now over two years old this fishery has settled down and fishes very well at most times. There are only 20 concrete pegs so come early at weekends to get a good one, peg one never fails!. It has two islands to target and a depth of around five feet. The bankside planting has now grown adding more features to target. This is a clean, well run fishery.

Types of Fish: Carp up to 14lb, bream to 3lb, tench to 4lb perch to 2lb. Other species include roach, orfe, ide, chub, rudd, and barbel.

Rules/Bans: Barbless hooks only, no keepnets.
No cat or dog food.

Number of Lakes: One

Facilities:

 22

Telephone: 0114 2815483   mob 07718 512958

Crookes Valley Park Lake
Crookes Valley Park, Crookesmoor, Sheffield.

Ticket Price: Free

Directions: From the centre of Sheffield, take the A57 Manchester Road. You will see signs for the university. At the university roundabout, take the third exit, which is Bolsover Street. Follow this road until you come to Winter Street and then onto Crookes Valley Road, you will see the park on your left hand side.

Description: This water covers just over 3 acres and has a concrete path all the way round providing plenty of places to fish. Depths vary all over this lake and in some places it is very deep, just under 30ft. Around the steps seems to be the most popular area to fish. It is rumoured that a 6ft catfish patrols the depths!

Types of Fish: There are plenty of carp in this lake and a few run up to 28lbs. Quality roach and perch are present, the larger ones approaching 2lb. Bream up to 3lb. There's also a few large chub nearing the 7lb mark.

Rules/Bans: No night fishing, no keepnets.
Park bylaws apply.

Number of Lakes: One

Facilities:

Telephone: Sheffield Council

15

Dam Flask Reservoir
Dam Flask Reservoir, Sheffield.

Ticket Price: £3.00, £2.00 for disabled, OAPs, and under 16s. Tickets purchased from a machine in the car park.

Directions: From Sheffield take the A57 towards Manchester. Then take the B6077 Loxley Road towards Bradfield, when you see the dam wall turn left.

Description: Situated about 7 miles outside Sheffield, it covers 115 acres, so if you like your solitude while fishing this water is for you. There is a road that runs the full way around the reservoir making access from your car easy. The water has a wide variety of depths with about six feet at the inlet to almost 100 feet at the dam wall, but the majority of the water averages between 15 and 20 feet.

Types of Fish: Bream averaging 2 to 3lb. Chub up to 6lb and perch to 4lb. A few tench and roach can be found. Pike run to around 34lb.

Rules/Bans: No keepnets, no ground bait, no night fishing, no live baits.

Number of Lakes: One   **Facilities:**   P

Telephone: 0114 2844219 or 07952 485798

Elsecar Reservoir

Elsecar Reservoir, Elsecar, Barnsley.

Ticket Price: £3.00, Juniors £2.00, OAPs free.

Directions: Exit the M1 at Junction 36 and follow the signs for Hoyland (A6135). After about a mile turn left onto the B6090. After you go over the hill turn left into Borrowfield Lane just before the village of Wentworth. Follow the road untill you reach the reservoir.

Description: This 12 acre reservoir has only got 28 pegs, with an average depth of four feet along the roadside. You can catch plenty of roach and bream that reach double figures using a waggler or pole about 12 meters out. There are some carp that weigh in at around 28lb.

Types of Fish: Carp, tench, roach, perch, bream,

Rules/Bans: Bloodworm, joker, and hemp. No night fishing.

Number of Lakes: One

Facilities: None

Telephone: 01226 743933

Forge Dam

Brookhouse Hill, Fulwood, Sheffield.

Ticket Price: Free fishing

Directions: Head out of Sheffield on the A57, signposted to Manchester. At the university follow the sign for Fulwood. As you reach the shops at Fulwood, turn left on to Brookhouse Hill. The dam and park are at the bottom of the hill.

Description: The dam is a short walk from the small parking area at the bottom of the hill, with a steep climb at the end to reach the water. This dam has unfortunately silted up alot over the last few years leaving the dam wall as the only area to fish from. This very picturesque dam has a great cafe with good food. Not suitable for the disabled angler.

Types of Fish: The biggest and most commonly caught fish are bream, which can go up to 5lb. Perch and roach are present with plenty of brown and rainbow trout.

Rules/Bans: Barbless hooks only. No night fishing

Number of Lakes: One

Facilities:

Telephone: 0114 2734481

Graves Park Pond
Meadowhead, Sheffield.

Ticket Price: Free.

Directions: From the centre of Sheffield take the A61 signposted to Chesterfield. The pond is in Graves Park which is on the left just before Meadowhead roundabout.

Description: This council run pond is surrounded by mature trees with average depths of only 4 feet. This small lake offers plenty of species for the beginner to tackle, especially roach. Fishing with a pole or whip on the drop will catch loads of perch if you feed little and often.

Types of Fish: Roach, perch, carp, tench and chub.

Rules/Bans: None

Number of Lakes: One

Facilities:

Telephone: 0114 2734481

Hillsborough Park Lake
Penistone Road, Sheffield.

Ticket Price: Free Fishing

Directions: From the centre of Sheffield take the A61 (Penistone Road). Turn left at Parkside Road, then immediately left into the carpark. The Lake is within Hillsborough Park which is just before Hillsborough football ground.

Description: This Sheffield Council run lake is around two acres in size. Fishing is from a concrete path that surrounds the lake. There are three islands to target, and most anglers were fishing close up to these. The water is shallow only three feet in most places. The only other problem is the large quantities of geese and ducks that live on the islands.

Types of Fish: Carp, tench, perch, roach and crucian carp.

Rules/Bans: No keepnets. Barbless hooks only.

Number of Lakes: One

Facilities:

Telephone: 0114 2734481

Howbrook Dam.
High Green, Sheffield.

1/2 PRICE VOUCHER *AT BACK OF BOOK*

Ticket Price: Day Tickets £3.00,
Season tickets available at £20.00. Concessions £12.00.

Directions: Exit the M1 at Junction 36 and head towards Sheffield on the A61. After about a mile you will find the dam on the right. Parking is on the long lay-by.

Description: This dam is about 4 acres in size and has plenty of features to target. Depths vary from 4 feet at one end to over 18 feet at the dam wall. With forty pegs to choose from, many being concrete flags or well built wooden platforms. The dam wall is where I found plenty of tench and carp. Big shoals of bream can be found with the largest fish at around 5lb. The water also has a good head of crucian carp with roach and rudd also present. This venue is not suitable for disabled anglers as access can be tricky. Recently restocked with 1000 rudd, 200 tench and crucian.

Types of Fish: Carp, tench, bream, crucian carp, roach, rudd

Rules/Bans: No night fishing. No bloodworm or joker

Number of Lakes: One

Facilities:

 9

Telephone: 0114 2465136 or 0777 3482033

KJS Aston Ponds
Aston, Sheffield.

£1.00 OFF VOUCHER AT BACK OF BOOK

Ticket Price: Day ticket £5.00.
OAPs £3.00 Mon-Fri £40 year permit.

Directions: From junction 31 of the M1, take the A57 towards Sheffield. At the roundabout turn left heading towards Killamarsh. Turn left after a few metres and follow the lane to the ponds.

Description: Ponds 1 and 2 formerly known as Laycocks Ponds are the first two ponds you come to. The first and biggest of the two has recently been stocked with 500 chub. This lake has a good head of bream and some big carp to 27lb. Twenty six pegs on the woodland bank are used for matches. The newly built platforms are excellent to fish from, plus the new cafe is very reasonable.

Types of Fish: Carp up to 27lb, bream, roach, ide, chub, rudd, and barbel.

Rules/Bans: Barbless hooks only, keepnets in matches only. No ground bait except in pole cup or feeder.

Number of Lakes: Two

Facilities:

Telephone: 0114 2470876

KJS Fisheries

KJS Fisheries, Station Road, Killamarsh.

£1.00 OFF VOUCHER AT BACK OF BOOK

Ticket Price: Day tickets are £5.00.
Year permits £50. OAPs £3 mon-fri

Directions: From Sheffield head for Mosborough on the A6135. At the main junction in Mosborough turn left, signposted to Killamarsh. Turn right straight after going under a bridge on to Station Road. You will find the fishery at the end of the road.

Description: This well run fishery has four waters to chose from, all with a superb range of fish. Lake 1 has a mix for coarse fish with 21 pegs. You will find more tench and crucian in lake 2 which has 30 pegs. Lake 3 is the carp lake with fish up to 20lbs. There is also a small stretch of canal.

Types of Fish: Roach, perch, rudd, tench, carp, and bream.

Rules/Bans: No keepnets except on canal section.
Barbless hooks only.

Number of Lakes: 3 Lakes, 1 Canal.

Facilities:

Telephone: 0114 2470876

26

Lewden Spring Fishery

Station Rd, Worsbrough Dale, Barnsley.

1/2 PRICE VOUCHER AT BACK OF BOOK

Ticket Price: Day ticket £5.00

Directions: From Junction 36 of the M1 take the A61 heading for Barnsley. When you reach Worsbrough turn right onto West street (A6100). After about a mile take your first right onto Station Road. Follow the road down the hill, when you reach a small bridge, the fishery is on your right.

Description: A very attractive and well run fishery which is set in woodlands just outside Worsbrough. It has 40 pegs all with platforms. The best place to catch is close to the large island in the middle. Make a note that they are shut on Tuesdays to let the fish recover from matches.

Types of Fish: Extensively stocked with crucian carp, ide, roach, tench, bream, rudd and carp up to 24lbs.

Rules/Bans: Barbless hooks only. No keepnets.

Number of Lakes: One

Facilities: Refreshments at the weekend between April and October

Telephone: 01226 249174

Loxley Fisheries

Loxley Road, Loxley, Sheffield.

FREE VOUCHER
AT BACK OF BOOK

Ticket Price: Day Tickets £5 After 3pm £4 After 6pm £3

Directions: The fishery is approached off the main Loxley road by taking the second left after passing the Admiral Rodney Pub on your right. The fishery is signposted at the top of the lane, and access is gained through the water treatment plant and the old Marshalls brickworks.
Drive through the works to the car park near the lake.

Description: Pegs 8 or 9 are the favourites, targeting the carp at the side of the lily pads. Surrounded by mature trees and with numerous bank side features this is a very attractive lake. With only 32 pegs to chose from it can get busy on match days leaving only a few pegs for pleasure anglers.
I Like to fish close-in going for the recently stocked barbel.
This well run fishery has got to be worth a visit.

Types of Fish: Large carp, roach, tench, perch, chub and barbel.

Rules/Bans: Barbless hooks only, no bloodworm, joker, boilies, or ground bait. Keepnets only in matches.
No night fishing.

Number of Lakes: One

Facilities: [P] [☕] [♿] **Some** bait sold on site.

Telephone: 0114 2864717 or 07831 720011

`17`

Milton Ponds
Hoyland, South Yorkshire.

1/2 PRICE VOUCHER AT BACK OF BOOK

Ticket price: Day tickets are £3.00.

Directions: Exit the M1 at Junction 36 and head towards Sheffield on the A6135. When you reach Hoyland, turn left at the traffic lights. When you pass the railway bridge, after about a mile you will see the fishery on the left hand side.

Description: You have the choice of two ponds with the smaller one being about 8 foot deep and mainly holding bream and roach. The top pond which is just behind the first pond you see, has plenty of carp and is ideal for small club matches with just over 20 pegs. These ponds are definitely worth a go especially on those warm summer evenings. Recently re-stocked with crucian carp and tench.

Types of Fish: Roach up to 2lb, rudd and carp, tench to about 5lb, plenty of bream and crucian.

Rules/Bans: No bloodworm, joker, boilies.
Keepnets only in matches.

Number of Lakes: Two

Facilities: ♿

Telephone: 01226 351059

More Hall Water Gardens

Manchester Rd, Bolsterstone, Sheffield.

2 FOR 1 FISHING VOUCHER AT BACK OF BOOK

Ticket Price: Day ticket £5.00, Concessions £3.00. Annual permits £30.00.

Directions: The lakes are between Oughtibridge and Deepcar on the A6102 Manchester Rd. It is easily found from the M1 motorway via junction 35a.

Description: There are four ponds at More Hall. The Corner Pond has 16 pegs and is stocked with ide, roach and carp. Keyhole pond has 10 pegs and has a variety of fish with carp up to 10lb. The other two new ponds both have 15 pegs. More Hall also has fishing rights to a section of the River Don which has excellent stocks of brown and rainbow trout, with barbel and chub present.

Types of Fish: Carp, rudd, bream, ide, tench, roach, trout, barbel, and chub.

Rules/Bans: Barbless hooks, no keepnets, no artificial baits

Number of Lakes: Four

Facilities:

Telephone: 0114 2883388 or 07703 107890
www.morehallwatergardens.co.uk

13

Nancy Pond
High Green, Sheffield.

Ticket Price: Day ticket £3.00

Directions: From Junction 36 of the M1 motorway take the A61 heading towards Sheffield. Cross the first roundabout you come to signposted Sheffield North. After a few hundred yards turn left into Greaves Lane. You will see a cattery on your left turn here and the pond is just up the hill.

Description: Recently de-silted this small 1/3 of an acre pond is well worth a visit, but in the summer months it could get busy with only 10 new pegs to fish from. Chapeltown and District AA run this pond and have introduced carp between 8oz and 3lb. You will also find a few tench along with ide, roach and perch.

Types of Fish: Carp up to 3lb, tench, perch, roach and ide.

Rules/Bans: Barbless hooks only, no keepnets, no bloodworm or joker. Ground bait in pole cups and feeders only.

Number of Lakes: One

Facilities: P

Telephone: 0114 2845424

Nether Mill Coarse Fishery
Barnsley Road, Penistone.

Ticket Price: Day tickets £5 available on the bank.

Directions: See Map

Description: Nether Mill is a mixed fishery with the emphasis on carp and bream. This one acre lake has three islands in it, and slopes quickly to around 6 feet. The 32 pegs are accessed by a path that runs all the way round making this very friendly for disabled anglers.

Types of Fish: Carp up to 19lb, bream to 7lb. Plenty of other species including roach, perch, tench, rudd, chub and crucian carp.

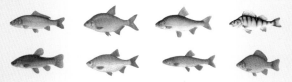

Rules/Bans: No keepnets, except during matches. No night fishing, no dogs, no barbed hooks. Also banned are nuts, cat meat and artificial baits.

Number of Lakes: One

Facilities:

Telephone: Adam Hinchliff 07770 670042

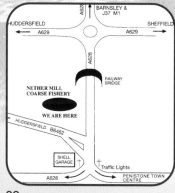

HUDDERSFIELD
BARNSLEY & J37 M1
SHEFFIELD
A629
A629
A628
RAILWAY BRIDGE
NETHER MILL COARSE FISHERY
WE ARE HERE
HUDDERSFIELD B6462
SHELL GARAGE
Traffic Lights
A628
PENISTONE TOWN CENTRE

Newbiggin Pond

A61, Lower Newbiggin, Barnsley.

FREE FISHING VOUCHER AT BACK OF BOOK

Ticket Price: Day ticket £2.50 Half day ticket £2.00

Directions: From Junction 36 of the M1 take the A61 heading for Sheffield. At the roundabout turn left onto the A616 heading back to the M1. After about a mile turn left into Park Lane and left again into the fishery carpark.

Description: A very attractive small pond with only 12 pegs, so to avoid disappointment arrive early. Two pegs are suitable for disabled anglers but it can be a bit noisy from traffic on the A616. The depth is around 7 feet all over the pond. It has been recently been re-stocked with 250 ide.

Types of Fish: Carp, tench, roach, perch, bream, crucian carp and ide.

Bans/Rules:

Number of Lakes: One

Facilities:

Telephone:
0114 2845424

NEWBIGIN RULES

1. Barbless hooks only (one hook only)
2. No keepnets
3. No bloodworm or joker
4. No litter
5. No live or dead baits
6. Groundbait in feeders and pole pots only
7. No fishing without a licence
8. No fires
9. No fish to be taken away
10. Juveniles under 12 years of age must be accompanied by an adult
11. landing net must be assembled before fishing

THANK YOU
C.D.A.A

Norwood Cottage Farm Fisheries
Killamarsh, Sheffield.

Ticket Price: Day tickets are £3.00 on the bank.

Directions: From Junction 31 of the M1, head towards Sheffield. At the first roundabout take a left turn. Keep going past the entrance to Rother Valley. When you reach a small roundabout turn left and go up the hill. You will come across a small turning on your left about a 1/4 of a mile up the hill. Follow the track to the fishery.

Description: This fishery is getting better with age and is already popular with match anglers. Two ponds to fish, with the larger one stocked with a wide variety of fish and has two islands. Depths vary from one end to the other. I prefer the shallower end near the stock pond, fishing close to the reed beds. Its well worth a visit to the new cafe

Types of Fish: Carp mainly in the 5-6lb bracket, with a few reaching 15lbs. Bream to 8lb. Tench to 5lb. Plenty of roach and perch to 1lb. Some small ide have been introduced.

Rules/Bans: Barbless hooks only. No floating baits. No keepnets except in matches.

Facilities:

Number of Lakes: Two

Telephone: Alwyn 0114 2489224

Pinch Mill Fisheries
Whiston, Rotherham.

1/2 PRICE VOUCHER AT BACK OF BOOK

Ticket Price: Day Tickets £3.50. Two rods £6.00.

Directions: Come of the M18 at Junction 1 and head towards Rotherham on the A631. At Worrygoose roundabout turn left and head for Thurcroft on the B6410. After a sharp left hand bend you will come across the fishery, around 200 yards on the left.

Description: There are two lakes to fish and both are tree lined making this a very attractive venue. Both ponds are of a similar size. The first one you come to has 26 pegs and is between 6 and 8 feet in depth. The other pond has 17 pegs and is shallower, around 4 foot. Most pegs are suitable for anglers with disabilities. Both ponds have recently been re-stocked with over a thousand carp.

Types of Fish: Both ponds contain plenty of ide that run to almost 3 pounds, but most average just over the 1 pound mark. There are a few carp present to 22lb, plenty of tench to 4lb, and barbell to 2lb. Good head of perch present.

Rules/Bans: No keepnets, barbless hooks only. No boilies, no trout pellets. Ground bait from pole cup or feeder only.

Number of Lakes: Two

Facilities:

Telephone: Rob 07855 312963

Rivelin Dam
Rivelin Valley Road, Sheffield.

Ticket Price: Free

Directions: From Sheffield city centre head towards Hillsborough on the A61. Turn left before Hillsborough Park and head towards Malinbridge. At Malinbridge turn left on to the A6101 Rivelin Valley Road. The dam is about a mile on your righthand side.

Description: Although very shallow this council run pond is worth a visit purely because of the high number of fish present. There are no pegs, fishing is from the path that goes around half of the pond, but this can get busy with walkers at the weekend.

Types of Fish: Roach, perch, tench and carp

Rules/Bans: None

Number of Lakes: One

Facilities:

Telephone: 0114 2734481

33

Rother Valley Country Park

Mansfield Rd, Wales Bar, Sheffield.

Ticket Price: Day ticket £3.15 Concessions £1.55.
Annual season ticket £50.65 Concessions £32.15

Directions: From the M1 Motorway Junction 31, follow signs to Sheffield city centre. At the first roundabout turn left onto the A618. Rother Valley is on the right after 2 miles.

Description: There are three places to choose from, Northern Lake, Nethermoor Lake and a long stretch of the River Rother. The two lakes contain plenty of perch, roach and carp, but many anglers prefer to fish the river where there has been some large chub caught.

Types of Fish: Carp, bream, chub, tench, roach, rudd and perch.

Rules/Bans: No ground baiting. Keepnets must not be used during March to June. Barbless hooks only.

Number of Lakes: Two + The River Rother.

Facilities:

Telephone: 0114 2471452

Roundwood Ponds
Aldwalke, Rotherham.

Ticket Price: £3.00 per day. Concessions £2.00

Directions: From the centre of Rotherham head towards Doncaster on Fitzwilliam Road. When you reach a large roundabout called the Mushroom roundabout, take your first left on to Aldwalke Lane. Continue to the last entrance to Corus steel works and follow the lane down to the ponds.

Description: Two ponds to chose from; one large pond with 30 pegs, and the other fairly small with 20 pegs.
The large pond boasts very good carp up to 31lb with plenty of quality tench. The best place to fish is in the nearest corner of the largest pond. It is sometimes difficult to reach the ponds but it is well worth the struggle, as the fishing is excellent.

Types of Fish: Carp to 30lb, tench to 8lb, pike up to 9lb, roach to 2lb, perch to 3lb, rudd and crucian.

Rules/Bans: Barbless hooks only, no keepnets in closed season, no pellets or paste, no boilies.

Number of Lakes: Two

Facilities: None

Telephone: 01709 561760

Underbank Reservoir.

Underbank Reservoir, Stocksbridge.

1/2 PRICE VOUCHER
AT BACK OF BOOK

Ticket Price: Day tickets £3.00.
Pike fishing £4.00 per rod

Directions: From Sheffield head towards Stocksbridge on the A616. You can't miss the reservoir just on the edge of Stocksbridge.

Description: Like most reservoirs in South Yorkshire it has plenty of depth, which provides anglers with good all year round fishing. If you like pike fishing then this is the water for you. Underbank also has a healthy stock of silver fish that are great sport. Many anglers come here for the bream which tend to catch better in the early morning.
A big favourite for piking from October to March

Types of Fish: Plenty of pike plus perch and roach to a pound, lots of carp, bream and tench.

Rules/Bans: All necessary equipment required for pike fishing

Number of Lakes: One

Facilities: None

Telephone: 07976 797158

Westwood Reservoir
High Green, Sheffield.

Ticket Price: Day Tickets £3.00. £20 a year starting in March

Directions: From the M1 Junction 36, head towards Sheffield on the A61. When you reach High Green turn left on to Wortley Road. After a short distance turn left into Westwood Road. Turn next right into Downland Avenue and follow this road to the bottom where you will find the reservoir.

Description: This is an excellent all year round venue. Great for roach in the colder months. Like a lot of reservoirs this one is very deep and can reach over 19 feet in places. A great water to fish with plenty of species to target, however it has only got 40 pegs and can get busy especially on match days. A few pegs near to the car park are suitable for the disabled angler as further along the bank it becomes fairly steep.

Types of Fish: The largest bream are just under 6lb. There are also plenty of chub present up to 5lb. The other main species are carp which reach 21lb. Tench nearing 5lb.

Rules/Bans: No keepnets, barbless hooks only. No bloodworm or joker.

Number of Lakes: One

Facilities: ♿ P

FREE FISHING VOUCHER AT BACK OF BOOK

 10

Telephone: 0114 2845424

West End Fisheries

Boiley Lane, Killamarsh, Sheffield.

£1.00 OFF VOUCHER AT BACK OF BOOK

Ticket Price: £5.00 per day. Year permits £30.00 OAPs £3.00 mon-fri

Directions: At the main shopping area in Killamarsh turn up Bridge St, and turn right at the Nags Head public house. Keep going on this road till you get to the West End pub where you turn right, then immediately left onto Boiley Lane. Follow the track to an old railway bridge, turn right into the car park.

Description: This fishery has been well stocked with carp, roach, rudd, bream and tench. The lake has 50 pegs, some situated in an island in the middle of the lake and is suitable for match fishing. Targeting close to the small islands gives the best chance of catching.

Types of Fish: Carp, rudd, bream, tench, and roach.

Rules/Bans: Barbless hooks only. No keepnets. All anglers must use a landing net. No ground bait except in a cup or feeder. Under 16's must be accompanied by an adult.

Number of Lakes: One. (a new match lake is under construction)

Facilities: Cafe open in summer months

Telephone: 0114 2470876

 27

Wire Mill Dam Fishery

Whiteley Wood Lane, Sheffield.

1/2 PRICE VOUCHER *AT BACK OF BOOK*

Ticket Price: Day Tickets £3.50. Concessions £2.50. After 4pm £2.00. Year Permits £30. Concessions £20.

Directions: From the centre of Sheffield take the A625 (Ecclesall Road). Turn right on to Knowle Lane after passing the Prince of Wales Pub. Continue up Knowle Lane and turn right 600 metres past the Hammer and Pincers Pub. Follow the road for about 1 mile and you will find the dam and car park on your left.

Description: Great for beginners with plenty of roach. perch, tench, and a good head of crucian carp. There are also a few large carp, well into double figures. The dam is under new management and is looking better already. It is quite shallow at only 4.5 feet at its deepest. This dam is full of fish and during the summer months maggot or sweet corn will catch all day long. The high quality roach and perch also makes this water one of the best winter fishing venues in the area.

Types of Fish: Carp, roach, perch, tench, bream, crucian carp.

Rules/Bans: Barbless hooks only, no keepnets except in matches, no night fishing. Ground bait in pole cup or feeder only. No floating baits.

Number of Lakes: One   **Telephone:** 07809 172872

Facilities: 21

Worsbrough Canal
Worsbrough, South Yorkshire.

Ticket Price: £2.50 for the day.
£1.75 for disabled, OAPs or under 16s.

Directions: From the M1, Junction 36, take the A61 and head towards Barnsley. After passing the Button Mill Pub, at the next set of traffic lights, turn right onto the B6100. The canal is on the righthand side, opposite the Wharfe pub.

Description: At just over five foot deep this canal has some overhanging trees and reed beds. This well kept stretch of canal is about 260 yards long and has 45 pegs. The carp have grown and now reach double figures.

Types of Fish: Carp to about 10lb, chub to 4lb, bream and tench to 5lb, plenty of crucian to around 1lb, and lots of roach, perch and rudd.

Rules/Bans: Barbless hooks only, no keepnets, except in matches.

Number of Lakes: One

Facilities: None

Telephone: 01226 289714 mobile 0795 8683015

Worsbrough Reservoir

Barnsley, South Yorkshire.

Ticket Price: Day tickets are £3.00 on the bank.
Season tickets £22, £11 Concessions

Directions: Coming from Barnsley take the A61 south. When you get to Worsbrough go through a set of traffic lights and turn right into Worsbrough Mill Country Park, across the road from the Button Mill pub.

Description: There are 80 pegs to fish at Worsbrough, with trees to one side and stone banks to the other. The depths vary from shallows to around 15 feet at the dam head. This reservoir is fished by top match anglers all year round. Parking is pay and display at £2 all day.

Types of Fish: There are a lot of bream to the 5lb mark, roach to 2lb, lots of big perch. You can also find pike here with many to 14lbs in weight, plus some good quality tench. Recently re-stocked with carp now weighing upto 14lb.

Rules/Bans: No carp in keepnets, free running method feeder only. No bloodworm, joker or nuts.

Number of Lakes: One

Facilities:

Telephone: 01226 203090

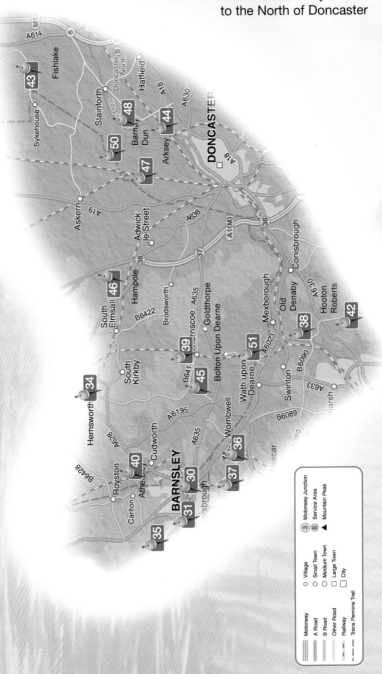

Fishlake

A614

A18

Hatfield

Doncaster (S) North

43

Sykehouse

Stainforth

48

Barnby Dun

44

Arksey

50

DONCASTER

A630

A18

47

Askern

A19

Adwick le Street

A638

A1(M)

36

Conisbrough

38

37

46

Hampole

South Elmsall

B6422

Brodsworth

A635

Goldthorpe

A630

Mexborough

Old Denaby

Hooton Roberts

42

Barnburgh

39

Bolton Upon Dearne

51

A6023

38

South Kirkby

B641

45

Wath upon Dearne

Swinton

B6090

A633

34

Hemsworth

South Hiendley

A6195

Wombwell

B6089

Cudworth

A635

36

Elsecar

Royston

40

Athersley

BARNSLEY

30

37

A628

B6428

Carlton

31

Worsbrough

35

Legend:

Motorway	○ Village
A Road	○ Small Town
B Road	○ Medium Town
Other Road	☐ Large Town
Railway	☐ City
Trans Pennine Trail	
③ Motorway Junction	
⑤ Service Area	
▲ Mountain Peak	

Bolton Brickponds

Bolton Brickponds, Goldthorpe, South Yorkshire.

Ticket Price: Day tickets £3.00. Multi rods £6.00. Concessions £1.50, Multi £3.00.

Directions: Come out of Barnsley on the A635 heading towards Doncaster and turn off when you see a sign for Goldthorpe (B6098). Turn off right and follow the road through Goldthorpe and after a mile you will see the ponds on your left.

Description: There are 3 inter-connected ponds to fish and with water around 28 foot in places, it's great for all year round fishing. There is plenty of different swims to fish and a lot of open grass areas for picnics. Most pegs are accessible to disabled anglers.

Types of Fish: There are the occasional tench up to 8lb. Bream to 7lb, pike to 26lb, rudd, roach and crucian to 2lb. Plus a few chub.

Rules/Bans: No keepnets, barbless hooks only. Permit required for night fishing

Number of Lakes: Three

Facilities:

Telephone: 01709 898948

44

Crumwell Lane Pond

Kingsforth Lane, Thurcroft, Rotherham.

Ticket Price: Day tickets £3.00.

Directions: Come of the M1 at Junction 32 and take the M18. Exit at Junction 1 and turn right heading for Hellaby. As soon as you leave the roundabout turn right. Continue for 1 mile and you should find the pond on your righthand side.

Description: This long strip shaped pond is about an acre in size and is treelined down one side. It has recently been restocked with carp, bream and tench. Plenty of roach and perch are present plus some large carp that reach the mid twentys. There are 22 pegs to chose from, work has been done to make many of them ideal for the disabled angler.

Types of Fish: Tench, bream, carp, perch and roach.

Rules/Bans: Keepnets are allowed at all times. Barbless hooks only. No hemp, sweetcorn or bloodworm. No groundbait.

Number of Lakes: One

Facilities:

Telephone: 01709 543558 or 0777 4540459

Dearne Valley Park Lake
Barnsley, South Yorkshire.

Ticket Price: Day ticket £2.00 Concessions £1.00

Directions: From the centre of Barnsley take the A628 Pontefract road. After a couple of miles you will see a pub called the Old White Bear on your left hand side. Take the second turning on the left and follow down to the lake.

Description: Run by Hoyle Mill Angling Club this lake is a perfect depth for the pleasure angler at just over 4 feet in most places except for the odd trench going to about 6 foot. You can only fish the bigger of the two lakes as the smaller one is for breeding. Using a feeder is the best tactic to catch the larger carp nearer the two islands, but many anglers were catching well using a pole.

Types of Fish: Carp to the 26lb mark, plenty of roach, perch, chub, tench and bream.

Rules/Bans: No keepnets, barbless hooks only. No floating baits, no boilies.

Number of Lakes: One

Facilities:

Telephone: Hoyle Mill Angling Club.

Elm Tree Farm Fisheries

1 Elm Tree Farm Court, Hooton Roberts.

Ticket Price: £4.50, £2.50 after 4.00 pm,
£3.50 for under 15's and disabled. Matches £5.00

Directions: Take the A630 from Conisbrough to Rotherham.
When you reach Hooton Roberts take a right turn on to the
B6090. You will see the lakes on your left.

Description: This venue consists of two lakes. The smaller of
the two has 21 pegs and is called Hooton Hollows. It is a
well-established lake having been there for only 8 years.
The depth is about 6 feet throughout and will fish well at
most times of the year. The second larger lake is called
Horseshoe Lake and has over 40 pegs to choose from.
Both lakes are full of silver fish and armed with some
maggots you can't fail to catch, making this an excellent
venue for the pleasure angler.

Types of Fish: There are crucian to just under 3lbs. Carp can
reach 20lbs, but most average around the 3lb mark. There
are also plenty of chub and tench present between
4 and 5lb. Roach and perch to nearly 2lbs.

Rules/Bans: Barbless hooks only, no keepnets.

Number of Lakes: Two

Facilities:

Telephone: 01709 855219

Ferryboat Farm Fisheries
Ferryboat Lane, Old Denaby, Doncaster.

1/2 PRICE VOUCHER AT BACK OF BOOK

Ticket Price: Tickets £5.00.

Directions: From the A1 Junction 36 take the A630 to Conisbrough. At the traffic lights turn right and head towards Mexborough on the A6023. When you reach a small roundabout, go straight over. Take the second turning on the left, signposted to Old Denaby. When you reach the village, turn right onto Ferryboat Lane, keep going till you reach the fishery.

Description: This four acre lake offers a good selection of 69 pegs with plenty of room between them. There are now caravan and camping facilities on site, great for a long stay. The water depth is between 5-6 feet which is ideal for the many carp in here, some reaching 15lb in weight.

Types of Fish: The carp are mainly around the 4lb mark. There are plenty of roach, perch and rudd. Some very good tench can be caught in this lake, around the 9lb mark. Bream and chub are also present.

Rules/Bans:

Number of Lakes: One

Facilities:

Telephone: 01709 588088 or 07930 958605

48

Fleets Dam
Fleets Dam, Barnsley.

£2.00 OFF VOUCHER AT BACK OF BOOK

Ticket Price: Day Tickets £6.00. Concessions £5.00. Year Ticket £80.00 Concessions £60.00

Directions: Take the A61 from Barnsley heading towards Wakefield. After about a mile take a left turn into Smithies Lane. Follow the road to the bottom of the hill and the dam is on the left hand side.

Description: The depth varies a lot on this water which favours the all year round angler. The bank closest to the car park is the shallowest at just over 4 feet. There is also a feature of a sunken wall about half way up the lake. This can often be one of the better places to fish. This dam is around 10 acres and has 75 pegs to choose from.

Types of Fish: Carp to about 17lb, but roach and bream are the main species here. There's a few chub and plenty of tench present, plus the odd pike in the mid twenties.

Rules/Bans: Barbless hooks only, no boilies or nuts.

Number of Lakes: One

Facilities: P

Telephone: 01226 292579

Grange Farm Lake

Grange Farm Lake, Fishlake, Doncaster.

Ticket Price: Day tickets at £5.00, concessions at £3.50.

Directions: Leave the M18 at Junction 6, and head east towards Stainforth. Follow the signs for Fishlake, the farm is signposted from the road.

Description: This lake is now a few years old and is getting better all the time. It has 40 pegs and is very well stocked with a variety of species, making this lake ideal for the beginner to catch nets full of fish. Feeding a little and often with maggot or caster is your best bet. The small island and bankside features offer plenty of areas to target.

Types of Fish: There are plenty of carp, with a few larger ones into double figures. There is a good stock of tench, roach, chub and bream.

Rules/Bans: Barbless hooks only, no cat or dog meat, no boilies, nut, or trout pellets. Children under 16 must be supervised.

Number of Lakes: One

Facilities:

Telephone: 01302 846163

Long Pond, Barnby Dun

Barnby Dun, South Yorkshire.

Ticket Price: Day tickets are £2.00.

Directions: Drive out of Barnby Dun and take Fordstead Lane heading towards Arksey. Turn right straight after driving over the River Don. The only parking is on the road side near the pond.

Description: This stretch of canal was part of the River Don a long time ago. It is a 56 peg stillwater and is packed with most species, including skimmers best caught on a pole with maggot, caster or soft pellet. Depths can vary between 4 $\frac{1}{2}$ feet in the shallow to 13 feet in the middle.

Types of Fish: Tench to 10lb, bream 6lb, perch 2 1/2lb, roach 3lb, pike to 17lb, plus a few carp.

Rules/Bans: No keepnets, barbless hooks only. No boilies.

Number of Lakes: One

Facilities:

Telephone: 01302 856249 (evenings)

Lowfield Lakes

off Station Rd, Bolton Upon Dearne.

1/2 PRICE VOUCHER AT BACK OF BOOK

Ticket Price: Day tickets £5.00, OAP's, disabled anglers and under 16's £4.00. Match £6.00.

Directions: The lakes are on the Goldthorpe to Bolton road. When you reach Bolton Upon Dearne, turn left into Station Road. After the railway bridge the road joins with Lowfield Road. The fishery is on the right.

Description: With three lakes to choose from at Lowfields there is plenty of room to fish, but the shape of them suits the pole angler as they are all strip ponds. The top lake has around 30 pegs with a variation in depth from 7 feet on one side to 4 feet on the other. The middle lake is wider with 17 pegs and not as deep, between 4-5 feet in most areas. Inner strip lake is the last of the ponds. Again it is fairly shallow at only 5 feet at its deepest.

Types of Fish: Carp are present in all three ponds with some over 21lbs in the top lake, but most are between 2 to 9lb. Tench to 8lb, bream to 9lb, roach and perch between 1 and 2lbs. Ide and a few rudd are also present.

Rules/Bans: No keepnets, except for matches. Barbless hooks only. No night fishing.

Number of Lakes: Three

Facilities:

Telephone: 01709 888470 or 07970 171499

 45

New Junction Canal
Barnby Dun to West End.

Ticket Price: Day tickets £3.00. Books are valid from April 1st 2007 at £17.00. Concessionary rates £10.00 available for OAP's and Juniors.

Directions: All fishing to take place on the west bank, except from Peg 422 to Peg 441 which are on the east bank. All stretches are clearly signposted. When one bank is matched under no circumstances is anyone allowed to fish the opposite bank.

Description: The canal is wide, around 30 metres, with distinct shelves at around 3m from each edge. The top of the ledges is only a few feet deep, but the main channel is around 7 to 10 feet deep making it fishable through winter. There is the odd bush and reed bed to be found creating fish holding features. The main species are Roach and Perch to around 1lb, but eels, chub and bream can put in an appearance if you're in the right place at the right time.

Types of Fish: Bream, perch, roach, chub and eels

Rules/Bans: Barbless hooks only. No vehicles on banks

Number of Lakes: One

Facilities: None

48

Telephone: 07771 986849

Information kindly supplied by Doncaster & District Angling Association.

The Canal is straight, wide and full of fish.

You'll get a little boat traffic, but it won't disturb your fishing.

There are a few bankside features to be found.

Plumpton Pond
Wombwell, Barnsley.

Ticket Price: Day ticket £4.00 Concessions £2.00

Directions: From Junction 36 of the M1, take the A6095 signposted Wombwell. After about 3 miles, at the fifth roundabout, turn left onto the B6096. Follow the road through Wombwell and turn left onto the A633. After ½ a mile turn right into Bradberry Balk Lane and the lake is a ¼ mile on your right.

Description: This very attractive lake is set within Netherwood Country Park. At ¾ of an acre in size and with a depth of about 5 feet this is a great lake for the beginner and experienced angler. There are 26 pegs to chose from and a good sized island to target.

Types of Fish: Bream, tench, carp.

Rules/Bans: Barbless hooks only. No keepnets.

Number of Lakes: One

Facilities: None

Telephone: 01226 211209

Sally Walsh's Dam
Hoyle Mill Rd, Hemsworth, Barnsley.

Ticket Price: Day ticket £3.00, Concessions OAPs £1.50. Night fishing for carp £7.00 by arrangement.

Directions:

Description: This mixed coarse fishery has plenty for every angler, especially for the carp fisherman, with some of the largest fish in South Yorkshire recorded in this dam. The water is surrounded by trees and has lots of reed beds to target close to the bank

Types of Fish: Common carp, mirror carp, bream, tench, roach, and perch.

Rules/Bans: Keepnets to be used only during matches. Barbless hooks only. No nuts.

Number of Lakes: One

Facilities: None

Telephone: 01226 203090

Smithies Reservoir
Barnsley, South Yorkshire.

Ticket Price: £3.00 a day, concessions £1.50.
Under 12's free accompanied by an adult.
Season Tickets £20.00 from April to April.

Directions: From Barnsley head towards Wakefield on the A61. After only half a mile from Barnsley town centre take a left turn into Smithies Lane. Follow the road to the bottom and you will see the water on your righthand side.

Description: The reservoir is in a dip and surrounded by trees. This makes it ideal for fishing on those windy days. Open all year round and with depths averaging 8 feet, this water fishes well in winter. The carp catch well on meat as do the tench. Caster and maggot are ideal for the roach and perch. Good condition pegs make it suitable for disabled anglers

Types of Fish: Lots of bream up to 6lbs, plenty of small carp, but still a few big ones coming in at around 27lb. Tench to 6lb, perch and roach make up the remaining species.

Bans/Rules: Barbless hooks only, no keepnets, except in matches.

Number of Lakes: One

Facilities: None

Telephone: 01226 203090

South Yorkshire Navigation Canal
Doncaster to Long Sandall.

Ticket Price: Day tickets £3.00. Books are valid from April 1st 2007 at £17.00. Concessionary rates £10.00 available for OAP's and Juniors.

Doncaster & DAA control full fishing rights on this water wherever it may be sought from below Sprotborough Weir to the railway bridge below Sandall Lock

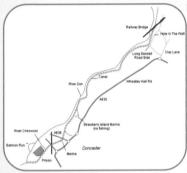

Description: The canal runs parallel to the River Don where the river isn't navigable. The water is split into two sections. The largest water runs from above the prison at Doncaster and for a few miles to the railway bridge near Long Sandal Lock. The second section runs from the swing bridge at Barnby Dun for about a mile before it splits to form the New Junction Canal and the Stainforth and Keadby Canal. The width is around 25 metres and depth is around 8 feet down the track. roach, skimmers, hybrid's, perch and gudgeon are the most common fish, but chub and bream can show occasionally.

Types of Fish:

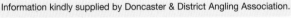

Facilities: None

Telephone: 07771 986849

44

Information kindly supplied by Doncaster & District Angling Association.

You can park right behind your peg at Long Sandall

Barnby Dun Swing Bridge

The Canal near Barnby Dun. Thorpe Marsh Power Station in the background.

Stubbs Hall Lakes

Stubbs Hall Farm, Hampole, Nr Doncaster.

Ticket Price: Day tickets are £5.00

Directions: Leave the A1 at the Redhouse junction, and join the A638 heading to Wakefield. In about two miles you should see a signpost for the fishery on your left.

Description: This fishery has 2 lakes, one is reserved for fly fishing the other is for coarse fishing. This clean, well maintained site has good access all round the lakes, ideal for the disabled angler. Both lakes are about three acres in size but beware they are very exposed to the wind. There are 46 good pegs and two islands in the coarse lake.

Types of Fish: I am told there are as many as six different types of carp in the coarse lake. The smaller carp are between 3 and 6lb, the largest one was recorded at 34lb. There are also some good sized tench and chub. Roach, bream and perch make up the remaining species.

Rules/Bans: Keepnets, only in matches. Barbless hooks only. All litter must be removed off site.

Number of Lakes: Two

Facilities:

Telephone: 01302 722739 / 07771 523128

46

Tinkers Pond

Tinkers Pond, Barnsley, South Yorkshire.

Ticket Price: Day Tickets £3.00, Concessions at £1.50.

Directions: From Barnsley city centre head towards Huddersfield on the A635. When you pass Barnsley College turn right on to Woodstock Road. Follow the road to the end, go under the railway bridge, and you will find the ponds on your right.

Description: There are two very similar ponds to choose from, except for the depths. The first water known as Top Pond ranges between 4 feet and 12 feet at its deepest. The other pond coincidentally called Bottom Pond, is much shallower reaching only 6 feet. I found fishing close-in produced good bites every time (mostly tench). This fishery has specially designed pegs for wheelchair anglers.

Types of Fish: Carp averaging 4lb with the biggest around 20lb. Tench go to 6lb. Bream at 4lb. Plenty of roach (2½lb) and perch 4lb.

Rules/Bans: Keepnets to be used only during matches. Barbless hooks only.

Number of Lakes: Two

Facilities:

Telephone: 01226 203090

Willow Garth Ponds

Shaftholme Road, Arksey, Doncaster.

1/2 PRICE VOUCHER AT BACK OF BOOK

Ticket Price: Day tickets are £4.00. Juniors £3.00. Evenings £3.00 / £2.00. Night fishing £8.00

Directions: Head towards Bentley on the A19. Turn right when you see the sign post for Arksey. Follow this road until you see a turn on to Shaftholme Lane. Cross over the railway line into Shaftholme Road, you will see the fishery on your right.

Description: The water is open throughout the year and does get busy during the summer months. Both lakes have plenty of features to fish. The carp and tench are the prominent species with the carp reaching 26lbs.

Types of Fish: Tench, roach, rudd, carp,

Rules/Bans: No keepnets, barbless hooks only.

Number of Lakes: Two

Facilities:

Telephone: 01302 563728

47

Wombwell Dam

Off Dovecliffe Rd, Wombwell, Barnsley.

£2.00 OFF VOUCHER AT BACK OF BOOK

Ticket Price: Day ticket £5.00 Concessions £4.00 £50.00 for the year.

Directions: From Junction 36 of the M1, take the A6095 signposted Wombwell. After about 3 miles, at the fifth roundabout turn left onto the B6096. Take your first left into Dovecliffe Road. After half a mile turn left onto a dirt track and the dam is at the end.

Description: There are two waters to fish at Wombwell Dam. The main dam depth varies between 3 and 24 feet, with plenty of carp over 10lb. The smaller pond contains crucian carp and tench. Both are surrounded by woodland making this a very attractive place to fish.

Types of Fish: Carp, bream, tench, roach, and perch.

Rules/Bans: Barbless hooks only. Keepnets are banned during the close season.

Number of Lakes: Two

Facilities: None

Telephone: 01226 292579

Section C

East and south of Doncaster towards Worksop.

Fishlake

A614 M18

6
64 Thorne

69

Rainforth

Doncaster North S 5 1

River Don

Barnby Dun

Hatfield

56

71 Hatfield Woodhouse

Sandtoft

66

Woodsey

A630

A18

65

DONCASTER

4

Wroot

61

M18

A614

A18

Auckley

58 Blaxton

B1396

62

3

Finningley

A638

New Rossington

M18

B6094 A60

B6376

B6463

Tickhill

63 Bawtry

Maltby A631

A631

A1(M)

Scrooby

1

A634

A614

67

32

Oldcoates

34

A60

38

32

B6060

B6463

68 54 Dinnington

31

55

60 Kiverton Park

A57

M1

Harthill 57

Woodsall marsh

53 Woodall

A618

A619

59 Barlborough

30

52 Clowne

▬ Motorway	○ Village	③ Motorway Junction
▬ A Road	○ Small Town	Ⓢ Service Area
▬ B Road	◎ Medium Town	▲ Mountain Peak
▬ Other Road	☐ Large Town	
▬ Railway	☐ City	
▬ Trans Pennine Trail		

63

Bank End Fishery

Bank End Fishery, Finningley, Doncaster.

Ticket Price: Day tickets £5.00 Concessions at £4.00.

Directions: Take the A614 to Blaxton. When you come to the crossroads with the Blue Bell pub, turn right onto the B1396. The waters are on the righthand side.

Description: Bank End has a new 34 peg match lake which opened recently, stocked mainly with carp. The other two lakes of about 4 and 3 acres are open all year round. The excellent shop which sells locally produced goods has a cafe where you purchase day tickets. Most of the 120 pegs are suitable for anglers with disabilities. I prefer the smaller of the two lakes as it's more sheltered. I did well fishing close to some reeds with a 5 metre pole.

Types of Fish: Plenty of roach, perch, and rudd. There is also quite a few Chub present. The Skimmer bream are now reaching a good size. Loads of carp too.

Rules/Bans: No dogs or radios permitted. No carp in keepnets, no bloodworm, hemp or tares. No Ground bait, barbless hooks only.

Number of Lakes: Three   **Telephone:** 01302 770224

Facilities:

Candy Corner Fisheries

Candy Corner Fisheries, Wroot, Doncaster.

Ticket Price: Day tickets £5.00 Concessions at £4.00
Fishing from 7.30 am till 7.30pm.
Now open all year .

Directions: From Doncaster take the A638 to Bawtry and
follow the signs for Auckley. Turn left onto the B1396.
Straight over at the roundabout in Auckley then take the
first left signposted Wroot. After about a mile you come to
the water on your right, just before a sharp bend.

Description: There are 4 lakes to fish at this venue. The
largest water is known as AJ's and has 45 pegs with a
depth of around six feet. Oscar's lake which is smaller has
26 pegs and is also shallower, about five feet. This fishery is
stocked with a mixture of quality fish but the carp seem to
be the dominant species. This water is very well kept and
most pegs are suitable for disabled anglers.

Types of Fish: Carp running to over 30lb. Bream and tench to
9lb and 6lb. The rest of the stock is made up of roach,
perch, rudd and ide.

Rules/Bans: No keepnets, no ground bait, no boilies,
bloodworm or joker, barbless hooks only, nets must be
dipped, no litter.

Number of Lakes: Four   **Telephone:** 01302 775062

Facilities:

Harlesthorpe Dam
Clowne.

£1.00 OFF VOUCHER AT BACK OF BOOK

Ticket Price: Mon-Fri tickets £5.00.
Weekends £6.00. (£1 extra per rod)
Night fishing on island only, £15.00 ring for details.

Directions: From the M1 take the A619 to Clowne. At the crossroad in the centre of Clowne turn left onto the A618. The fishery is a few hundred yards, on both sides of the road.

Description: The main lake of about 10 acres is mainly stocked with carp up to 25lb, and with plenty over 10lb you are sure of good net weights. The depth can vary from 5 feet in the reeds to 14 feet in the middle. I prefer the smaller lake across the road that is surrounded by trees and has a variety of fish present, with good sized chub and tench.

Types of Fish: Carp, tench, chub, roach, bream, perch, and rudd.

Rules/Bans: No carp in keepnets, barbless hooks only.

Number of Lakes: Two

Facilities:

Telephone: 01246 810231

52

Harthill Fisheries

Harthill Fisheries, Harthill, South Yorkshire.

Ticket Price: This is now a syndicate water.
£30 per year daytime. £100 per year day+night.

Directions: Exit the M1 at Junction 30. Follow the signs for the village of Harthill. When you get to the roundabout in the village turn left onto Woodhall Lane. Left again into Pryor Mede. Drive through the gate to the car park.

Description: The three waters together cover around 20 acres, and offers something for all anglers throughout the seasons. The first lake you come to is the deepest approaching 22 feet near the wall. The other lakes are more fishable with the top lake being only 7 feet deep in the middle. The largest water is called The Boating Lake and is very open and is mainly fished with a feeder set up.

Types of Fish: The largest fish are the carp, which run to 28lb. There are some very good bream, with the bigger fish up 8lb. Tench run to about 5lb. Perch nearing 4lb, with roach to 2lb.

Number of Lakes: Three

Facilities:

Rules/Bans: No carp in keepnets.
Barbless hooks only. 2 rods max.

Telephone: 0772 4076050

Hatfield Water Park & Lake

Hatfield Water Park, Hatfield.

Ticket Price: Day Tickets £2.90 on the bank.
Concessions £1.50 for juniors.

Directions: On leaving Doncaster you need the A18 Thorne to Hatfield road. After about 5 miles you will come to the village of Hatfield. Pass through the village then follow the signs for the park which you will find on the left hand side.

Description: This water is run by Doncaster Council, and at a little over 22 acres and with depths of nearly 40 foot in the middle it can be slightly daunting at first to tackle. There is ample parking available which is near to the public toilets. The location is a popular leisure facility and can get busy at weekends with walkers and kids. In terms of waterside features there are plenty but very few fishable pegs.

Types of Fish: The water is stocked with mostly silver fish. There are plenty of tench here to with the larger fish caught at over 6lb. The bream run to $3\frac{1}{2}$lb, with some quality roach over $2\frac{1}{2}$lb and to top it off there are perch that can be caught in the region of 2lb in weight.

Number of Lakes: One   **Telephone:** 01302 841572

Rules/Bans: No keepnets, barbless hooks only.

Facilities:

Hayfield Fishing Lakes

Hayfield Lane, Auckley, Doncaster.

Ticket Price: Day Tickets £5 per peg. £6 per match peg, 7am till dusk

Directions:

Description: Hayfield Lakes are situated to the south of Doncaster in idyllic countryside, just south of Rossington Bridge. There are two large lakes; Adams Lake 82 pegs and Dannies Island Lake 79 pegs, both of which are stocked with a variety of fish. It is best known as the match fishing home of Fish O Mania.

Types of Fish: Carp, bream, orfe, roach, rudd, tench, barbel

Rules/Bans: No keepnets (except during matches) No night fishing. No barbed hooks. No hooks larger than a size 10. No dogs, litter, fires. No boilies.

Number of Lakes: Two   **Telephone:** 01302 864555

Facilities: 58

Horseshoe Lake
Forge Road, Wales, Sheffield. S26 5RS

Ticket Price: Day Tickets £5.00. (Tues-Sun) 7am till dusk.

Directions: Leave Sheffield on the A57 towards the M1, then turn onto the A618 signed for Killamarsh. Look for the sign for Wales and follow this into the village. Take a left turn into Manor Road, then 2nd right into Forge Road where the lake is situated.

Description: Two lakes to chose from totalling about 3 acres, The water is deepest towards the centre, but a rod length out will see the best part of 5 foot to fish in. There are plenty of facilities on the site including a cafe and toilets. Many of the 24 pegs are suitable for anglers with disabilities. The new Silver Lake has most species but if you want the larger ghost carp try the bigger lake.

Types of Fish: There are plenty of carp that average 3lb, the largest at around 17lbs. Many crucian to a pound and a half. Good size bream and perch, with roach, ide, rudd and tench present.

Rules/Bans: No keepnets (except during matches). No barbed hooks, no hooks larger than a size 12.
Permitted Baits: maggots, pinkie, squats, caster, blood worm, joker, worm, carp pellets, carp pellet paste, All other baits and ground bait are banned.

Facilities:

Telephone: 01909 773826   **Number of Lakes:** Two

Kiveton Farm Fisheries
Kiveton Lane, Todwick.

£2.00 OFF VOUCHER AT BACK OF BOOK

Ticket Price: Day tickets £5.00.

Directions: From the M1, Junction 31, head towards Worksop on the A57. At the first set of traffic lights, turn right on to Kiveton Lane and follow the road through Todwick, you will see the entrance to the farm on your left.

Description: Both ponds are a good size with 86 pegs to chose from. With depths of between 4 to 5 feet you catch virtually everywhere especially around the island in one of the lakes. The ponds have a mix of fish but the carp are what most anglers come here for, with the largest reaching around 21lb.

Types of Fish: Carp to just over 20lb. Barbel to around 7lb. Roach up to 2lb, tench to 4lb, and chub to just under 6lb.

Rules/Bans: No bloodworm, joker, boilies, no ground bait. Keepnets only in matches. No night fishing.

Number of Lakes: Two

Facilities:

Telephone: 0114 2864179

Kiveton Waters
Hard Lane, Kiverton Park.

Ticket Price: Day tickets £5.00. Concessions £3.00

Directions: From the M1, Junction 31, head towards Worksop on the A57. At the first set of traffic lights, turn right on to Kiveton Lane and follow the road to a T-junction. Turn left, then immediate right onto Hard Lane. After about half a mile you will see the lakes on your right.

Description: Kiverton Waters is a British Waterways fishery opened in June 2006. There are three lakes which total approximately 6.5 acres. One of them has been stocked with silver fish only and has 78 pegs, including disabled pegs. The other two have most species including some large carp.

Types of Fish: Tench, carp, roach, rudd and other silver fish.

Rules/Bans:

Fishery Rules

- Barbless hooks only, maximum size 12.
- Fishery nets only to be used.
- Ground bait in pole cups and feeders only.
- All feeders must be free running, no bolt rigs.
- No floating baits.
- Fishery feed pellets only to be used, maximum of 2 bags.
- No bait to be thrown in at the end of each session.
- No leaving litter.
- No tins allowed on pegs, all bait must be in bait tubs or bags.
- No washing cat meat in lakes must be done prior to arriving. (only 1 tin per session)
- No children under 14 years without adult supervision.
- Fishing 7am - dusk.

Number of Lakes: Three

Facilities:

Telephone: 07773 102488

Lindholme Lakes

Sandtoft, Doncaster.

Ticket Price: Day Tickets £5.00. Evenings £3.00 Children under sixteen £4.00

Directions: From the M180, Junction 2 head for Belton. Turn right at the roundabout and follow the road to Sandtoft. When you reach the roundabout in Sandtoft take the second left and continue for nearly a mile. The fishery is signposted on your right.

Description: Lindholmes popularity and size keeps growing with two more lakes being added in the last couple of years. This makes it one of the biggest in the county but it is still a well run and friendly fishery and not one to be missed. Willows and Laurels Lakes are very similar in size and shape and both have many species present. The Big Lake, which is over 150 years old, is where the best carp can be found.

Types of Fish: This water contains a variety of carp many up to 12lb, and a few big ones reaching 29lbs. There are also some very nice tench to 11lb in the Big Lake. Other species include roach, bream, chub, barbel, and pike .

Rules/Bans: No carp in keepnets, no dogs, no joker or bloodworm, barbless hooks only.

Number of Lakes: Eight (515 pegs) **Telephone:** 01427 872905

Facilities:

66

www.lindholmelakes.co.uk

Lodge Farm Fisheries
Scrooby Top, Doncaster.

1/2 PRICE VOUCHER AT BACK OF BOOK

Ticket Price: Day Tickets £5.00.
Concessions £4.00. Match £6.00

Directions: Come out of Bawtry heading south on the A638.
Lodge Farm is on the left just before Ranskill.

Description: Five great ponds at this venue with the top pond
having mixed coarse fish with 46 pegs and depths of
around 15 feet. The Lily Pond and Long Pond has mainly
carp, chub, and bream with around 30 pegs each.
Field Pond has 38 pegs with carp , bream, chub and barbel.
Signal Lake has also got carp, bream, chub and a good
head of tench. An excellent cafe has recently opened on
site and is worth a visit.

Types of Fish: Carp, chub, bream, tench, barbel and some
recently introduced ide.

Rules/Bans: No keepnets (except matches),
All nets must be dipped on site, Barbless hooks max size
12, no in line or running method type feeders, no nuts,
boilies, bloodworm or joker. All litter must be taken from site.

Number of Lakes: Five

Facilities:

Telephone: 0781 5030694

67

74

Pebley Reservoir

Pebley Reservoir, Harthill, Sheffield.

£2.00 OFF VOUCHER AT BACK OF BOOK

Ticket Price: Day Tickets £4.00.
Night fishing by arrangement £10.00.
Season tickets £65.00 April to April.

Directions: From Junction 30 of the M1, head towards Worksop on the A619. After a mile turn left onto the A618. The reservoir is a mile or so down this road.

Description: A new small pond has been created across the road from the 26-acre main lake. It's been stocked with carp to 15lbs, bream, roach and tench, well worth a visit if you prefer the smaller waters. The main lake is one of the largest waters in the area, with a water depth of between 9 and 24 feet. The shallowest area can be found near the car park, with the deepest being near the dam wall. This is a very attractive lake set in a wooded valley.

Types of Fish: The water carries a good stock of fish, with carp to 15lb. Plenty of tench to over 8lb, plus many more fish including bream over the 10lb mark. Great pike venue with matches run during the winter months.

Rules/Bans: No fixed rigs. Barbless hooks preferred. No fish over 3lbs in keepnets

Facilities: None   **Number of Lakes:** Two

Telephone: 0114 2514936 or 07779 813355
Killamarsh Angling Supplies

57

Riverside Fishery

Gibbet Lane, Bawtry, Doncaster.

£1.00 OFF VOUCHER AT BACK OF BOOK

Ticket Price: £5.00 per day, £4.00 Concessions £6.00 Matches, £5.00 Match Concessions

Directions: The fishery is located 2 miles north of the A1M roundabout at Blyth, 1 mile south of Bawtry on the A614.

Description: The lakes here have been completely restocked with a good variety of quality fish. Ricky's Lake has 45 pegs and new match record of 135lbs. Strip Lake has 10 pegs, and Sandmartin lake has 20 pegs also with a new match record of 112lbs. All the lakes have a depth of around 7 feet. The river next to the lakes can also be fished.

Types of Fish: Roach, bream, rudd, barbel, carp to 15lbs, chub and tench.

Rules/Bans: No keepnets, barbless hooks only.

Number of Lakes: Three

Facilities:

Telephone: 01302 711889

63

Straight Mile Fishery
Brampton, near Dinnington.

Ticket Price: Day ticket £5.00, Concessions £4.00.

Directions: From the M1 Motorway Junction 31 take the A57 to Worksop. Turn left at the first set of traffic lights. After about half a mile turn left again into Pocket Handkerchief Lane. At the end of the lane turn left and the fishery is on your left hand side.

Description: The lake is made up of four strips separated by three islands, with plenty of features to target. You will catch in the middle, near the islands or close in. This is an all year round fishery with 100lb nets recorded.

Types of Fish: Carp, bream, chub, barbel, roach.

Rules/Bans: Barbless hooks only.
Juniors Must be accompanied by an adult.

Facilities:

Number of Lakes: One

Telephone: 01909 561663

Thorne Delves Ponds
Delves Lake, Thorne.

Ticket Price: £2.50 a day. £1.50 concessions.

Directions: From Junction 6 of the M18 head towards Thorne on the A614. Once you have passed the railway bridge look out for the fishery on the right.

Description: A really good fishery to try with two lakes and plenty of features to target. Both lakes are stocked with most species and of about the same depth, around 7 feet at the deepest. However, I prefer the smaller of the two, fishing close to the island and catching every time. Roach and perch mainly but I had a couple of tench out. I think the larger lake does seem to be more for the carp angler.
They have added some more carp and ide to the ponds as well as finding a few eels while restocking.

Types of Fish: Perch, roach, tench, bream, ide, carp and eel

Rules/Bans: Keepnets in matches only, barbless hooks only. No bloodworm or joker. No nuts or wasp grub.

Number of Lakes: Two

Facilities:

Telephone: 01405 817294

Triangs Fishery

Tythe Farm, Kirton Lane, Thorne.

Ticket Price: Day Ticket £5.00

Directions: From the M180 Junction 1, take the A614 towards Thorne. Turn left just before the canal flyover and head towards Stainforth. Turn right just after crossing the railway lines into Kirton Lane. You need to open the gates to cross back over the railway line (ring from phone at side of track first). The fishery is few hundred yards on your left.

Description: Three excellent waters here; one is for year book holders only but there always seems plenty of room to fish. The water is situated next to Thorne Golf Club so watch out for golf balls. Willow ponds depths vary from 5 feet to 10 feet at its deepest and has a small island which when fished close to gives the best bites.

Types of Fish: Carp, tench. chub, bream, and roach.

Rules/Bans: No ground bait, boilies, nuts, cat or dog food. No night fishing. No dogs, all litter must be removed from fishery. Under 14s must be accompanied by an adult. Max hook size 10, barbless hooks only.

Number of Lakes: Three

Facilities:

Telephone: 01405 816402 or 07890 167407

Tyram Hall Fishery
Hatfield.

1/2 PRICE VOUCHER AT BACK OF BOOK

Ticket Price: Day tickets Carp Lake £6.00. 24hr £15. Coarse Lake £5.00

Directions: Heading South on the A18, take the A614 to Bawtry. Go through Hatfield Woodhouse and take a left at the hall.

Description: This popular fishery has four ponds and offers excellent sport all year round. The carp lake has some very large fish around the 30lb mark. The main coarse lake has plenty of silver fish, and either pole or feeder fishing will catch good net weights. There are some large pike at this fishery, weights up to 25lb have been landed. Try the smallest lake called Tench lake. It is usually the quietest, but as the name suggests there are plenty of tench to target.

Types of Fish: The Coarse lake has roach, perch, tench and bream. Many types of carp in the carp lake. A few large pike.

Rules/Bans: No keepnets, barbless hooks only.

Number of Lakes: Four

Facilities: New additions to the venue include a bar, indian restaurant and accommodation

Telephone: 01302 840886

65

Woodhouse Grange
Woodhouse Grange Lakes, Hatfield Woodhouse.

Ticket Price: Day tickets £5.00 from cafe.
Matches £5.00 for 5 hours, £6.00 for 6 hours.

Directions: From Bawtry head north on the A614.
Go through Blaxton and you will find the fishery on your right just before you reach Hatfield Woodhouse.

Description: There are six waters to choose from and another four under construction half a mile away. These are excellent ponds with plenty of quality fish to target. Everyone seemed to be catching on the day I went. Fishing at a poles length with a white maggot worked for me.

Types of Fish: Roach, perch, bream, carp and tench

Rules/Bans: No bloodworm or joker, no hempseed or tares, no boilies or nuts, no method feeder. Barbless 12 max hooks. No keepnets. Ground baits though small feeder or pole cup. All meats are now banned.

Number of Lakes: Six

Facilities:

Telephone: 07702 189657 or 07802 518612

Woodland Farm Fisheries

Ward Lane, Barlborough.

FREE FISHING VOUCHER
AT BACK OF BOOK

Ticket Price: Day tickets £5.00.
OAP's juniors £4.00.

Direction: From Sheffield head for Junction 30 of the M1. Just before the junction turn left, sign posted Barlborough Village. Ward Lane is on the left when you reach the shops. Follow the lane to the bottom where you will find the fishery.

Description: The fishery has something for everyone, with 82 pegs over four lakes there's plenty for match, pleasure and specimen anglers. Ice House Lake and Bluebell Lake contain the larger fish with carp to 26lbs. Island Pond holds carp to around 7lb with roach, orfe, ide, and skimmers. Kingfisher Lake has a mixture of silver fish and carp up to 15lb.

Types of Fish: Carp, rudd, roach, bream, ide, orfe.

Rules/Bans: Keepnets only in matches. No night fishing. Barbless hooks only

Number of Lakes: Four

Facilities:

59

Telephone: 0114 2653541 or 07771 851185

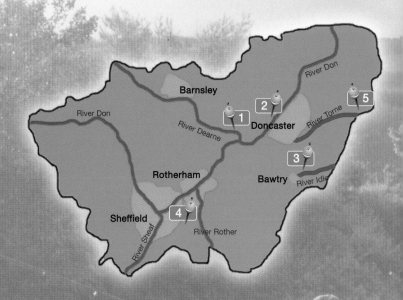

Barnsley

River Don

River Don

2

1

Doncaster

River Dearne

5

River Torne

River Don

3

Rotherham

Bawtry

River Idle

Sheffield

4

River Sheaf

River Rother

River Dearne, River Don, River Idle, River Rother, River Torne

This Environment Agency survey team member captured an 11lb salmon below Sprotborough weir on the River Don.

River Dearne
Denaby Main

Ticket Price: Day tickets £1.50. Season permit £6.00.

Directions: From the A1 follow the signs for the Denaby Main, carry on through Denaby Main up to the roundabout, go right at the roundabout over the River Don and canal and turn right at the ATS garage onto Pastures Road. Carry on down the road past the Pasture Lodge Motel, go over the River Dearne bridge 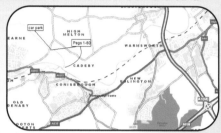 then turn immediately right into the car park. Finally go over the stile and you are on the banks of the River Dearne.

Description: This stretch of the River Dearne is run by the Denaby Miners Welfare Angling Club and comprises of 60 pegs from the Pastures Road Bridge to the confluence with the River Don at Denaby Main. Twenty species of fish have been recorded in the last few years. The dominant fish have been skimmers, hybrid's, roach, chub, perch, gudgeon, and dace. Chub to 3lb are a regular size catch. The highest pleasure fishing weight record is 49lbs 15oz consisting of 184 roach and a single skimmer caught with a waggler and caster.

Types of Fish: Bream, roach, perch, chub, dace, gudgeon and carp .

Telephone:
01709 864037

Information kindly supplied by the Denaby Miners Welfare A.C.

84

River Don

Doncaster, Hexthorpe and Sprotborough.

Ticket Price: Day ticket £3.00
Books are valid from April 1st 2007 at £17.00
Concessionary rates £10.00 available for OAP's and
Juniors.

Directions:

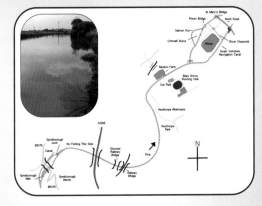

Description: Doncaster & D.A.A. control the fishing rights on
the Don from Sprotborough Weir and downstream to
Crimpsall Sluice near Doncaster Prison.

The river is deep, up to 15 feet down the centre, with a
width of around 30 metres. Because of the depth, fish can
be caught all year round. In fact it's not uncommon for big
bags on some of the colder winter days.

At usual level the river is slow, almost still at times, but be
careful when it's been raining. Because the banks are steep
the river is prone to rising quickly. Even a foot of extra water
will make the river very difficult to fish.

The main species to be caught are roach, skimmers, perch,
barbel and chub, but dace, bream, pike, eels and even carp
can be found.

The barbel average around 3 to 5 lbs but bigger fish have
been caught and they're getting bigger every year.

Bags of small fish can top 20lbs on a good day, but 10lbs is
still a good catch.

River Don, Hexthorpe

Sprotborough Weir

Eden Grove, Hexthorpe

Methods:

One of the great things about the River Don is that fish can be caught on the pole, stick float, waggler, topper, slider, groundbait feeder, bomb and almost any method you can think about. For the barbel try meat or pellet on the hook over a bed of hemp. If you can find a patch of gravel the barbel will find you.

For the chub, look for pegs with overhanging trees or a crease in the current. The classic combination of hemp and caster should do the trick.

For the roach and skimmer you can loose feed, but the depth means that is usually better to fish over a bed of groundbait. The pole is the obvious choice when the river is at normal level, but a float on running line is better when the river is up 6 inches or so. Try pinkies, maggots or caster.

Rigs:

If you're after the barbel or chub they can be had on the usual feeder or bomb setups, but don't discount the stick float or waggler. Try running a heavy float with plenty of shot down the line. You can drag up to a couple of feet along the bottom to slow the bait down as most pegs are snag free with a sandy bottom. Hooklengths should be around at least 3 to 4lb. Hooks should suit your bait size, but a size 14 will give you plenty of leverage should you hook a big 'un. The roach and skimmers can be a little cute, so you'll have to scale your rigs down, whether you use the pole or running line. Hooklengths as light as 1lb (0.006) are sometimes the only way you can get bites.

Rules/Bans:

No fires or camping allowed.
No night fishing. No live baits.
No cars or motorcycles allowed
on banks. No wasp grub.
Bloodworm and joker is only
allowed between Oct and March.
No litter to be left on banks.
Keep to recognised footpath.
Close all gates.

Types of Fish: Roach, perch, barbel and chub, bream, pike, eels and carp

Telephone: 07771 986849

Information kindly supplied by Doncaster & District Angling Association.

River Idle

Bawtry. Newington. Mission.

Ticket Price: Fishing is free on the Bawtry stretch of the Idle at Newington and Mission; day tickets are £2.50.

Directions: Bawty. Leave the A1 and take the A631 (Bawtry Rd) signposted Bawtry. Proceed through High Street and turn left onto Wharf Street. Park and take the footpath under the viaduct and follow this path to the left which will take you to the river.

Newington.
From Bawtry take the A164 heading to Finningley. When you reach Newington turn right at the Ship Inn and park.

Mission.
From Newington take Bawtry Road and after a mile or so you will reach Mission. Drive through the village and turn right into River Lane. Follow the lane to the river.

Description: The river in most places is between 12 and 20 feet wide, with depths from 4 to 7 feet. The water runs at an easy pace and I found using a stick float with a single red maggot worked well, but to avoid the gudgeon try a bit of corn. There's a very good stock of silver fish with roach over two pounds. Good size bream have been caught some to six pounds. Chub and perch make up the other dominant species. This river is also great for piking with some old ones reaching twenty pounds.

Types of Fish: Pike, roach, perch, chub, bream, gudgeon and dace.

3

River Rother
Catcliffe, Sheffield.

Ticket Price: Day ticket £2.00. Adult season tickets £10.00 OAP's and children under 16 £5.00. Children under 12 can fish for free if accompanied by an adult who is also fishing.

Directions: It is easy to find by car just off the M1 motorway, Junction 33, via the Sheffield Parkway to the village of Catcliffe. The river runs alongside Orgreave Road, with free parking at both ends of the fishery via The Plough public house.

Description: Who would have thought that the once most polluted river in the country a few years ago would have turned out to be a vastly improving fishery, well that's the Rother in Catcliffe. Catcliffe, Brinsworth and Treeton Anglers Alliance have control of a mile of river at Catcliffe, and believe me it produces some very good fish. Big perch the best up to now being a 4 pounder taken by Mick Kitchin in a match when he had eight perch for 21 pounds. There are also some very good chub, up to 5 pounds, with a few 2 pound roach. Some very good barble, carp and pike, dace and gudgeon, also trout up to 4 pounds.

There are 50 platforms, 23 of these are 4 foot wide and 5 foot long. These are ideal for the disabled angler.

The fishery offers many good aspects of fishing. Its diversity offers good sport to the many different types of fishing, with some very deep slow glides to faster shallow swims, making it ideal for float or ledger fishing, or spinning for pike, perch and trout.

Types of Fish: Pike, roach, perch, chub, barbel, carp, trout .

Facilities:

P   ♿

Telephone:
07774 884946

4

Information kindly supplied by Clive Nuttall Secretary of Catcliffe, Brinsworth, Treeton Anglers Alliance.

River Torne

Epworth Road Bridge to Pilfrey Bridge.

Ticket Price: Day ticket £3.00. Books are valid from April 1st 2007 at £17.00. Concessionary rates £10.00 available for OAP's and Juniors.

Directions: Epworth Road Bridge to Pilfrey Bridge on the A18 - a stretch of about 15 miles. Access may be gained at various road bridges.

IMPORTANT NOTICE

The River Torne Epworth Bridge to Belton Bridge

Please refer to the map. There is no vehicular access from Belton Bridge upstream past Dippings Farm towards Epworth Road Bridge. Anglers must park at Belton Bridge and walk upstream. Alternatively, anglers may drive downstream from Epworth Bridge, but not past Dippings Farm. Anglers using this

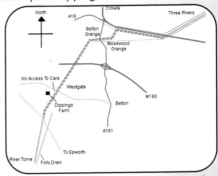

water must park off the track to allow the safe passage of farm vehicles and lorries. This track is Private Property. Please respect the owners wishes and the agreements that the Association has made with the owners.

Description: Technically this section is in North Lincolnshire. The river is more of a drain than a river and is close to the border with South Yorkshire. It's only around 13 metres wide but there is a little variety where sections of rushes extend into the water. Depth is around 4 or 5 feet. In summer the river can be slow, weedy and clear, but in winter the water is usually coloured due to water being pumped off the fields. Roach are the predominant species, but the river is probably most famous for it's pike population. Plenty of fish to over 20lbs are caught every year and jacks to mid singles are commonplace.

The River Torne at Belton Grange.

The River Torne near Mosswood Grange

Methods: For the pike deadbaits are king, but spinning comes a very close second.

Caster, punched bread or pinkie are the key baits for the roach. Hemp and tares can be great if you find big shoal of roach.

Pole fishing with a long line is often best but be careful of spooking the fish in the clear water.

Small amounts of loose feed should be fed regularly. If bites don't come quickly try feeding and fishing further downstream to draw the fish up, then bring them up the river by feeding back at your starting point

Rigs: Fish light rigs with No.11 shot or even better, No.9 leads spread out so that the bait falls naturally through the water at the same speed as your loose feed.

Many of your bites from the roach will come on the drop and will be sharp, so be alert.

Experiment with different feeding patterns until the bites become easier to hit.

Don't go too light with the lines because of the weed. Try around 1.5 to 2lbs with hooks around a size 22.

Types of Fish: Pike, roach, perch, tench, chub, and eels.

Rules/Bans:
No fires or camping allowed.
No night fishing. No livebaits.
No cars or motorcycles allowed
on banks. No wasp grub.
Bloodworm and joker is only
allowed between Oct and March.
No litter to be left on banks.
Keep to recognised footpath.
Close all gates.

Telephone: 07771 986849

Information kindly supplied by Doncaster & District Angling Association.

South Yorkshire Tackle Shops

Alan's Fishing Tackle, 111 Main St, Bramley, Rotherham, S66 2SE.	01709 702454
Bag-Up Angling Supplies, 16d Station Rd, Chapeltown, S35 2XH	0114 2466670
Bankside Tackle + Bait, 2 Balmoral Rd, Sheffield, S13 7QG.	0114 2692483
Bennetts Of Sheffield Ltd, 1 Stanley St, Sheffield, S3 8JP.	0114 2756756
Billy Clarke, 77-81 Alderson Rd, Sheffield, S2 4UB.	0114 2551145
Calcott's, 34-38 Wicker, Sheffield, S3 8JB.	0114 2722817
Carrilon UK, Hawks Nest, Great North Rd, Doncaster DN10 6AB.	01302 719933
Climax Fishing Tackle Ltd, 2 Stubley Hollow, Dronfield,	01246 291155
Dave Parkes Fishing Tackle, 46 Westgate, Rotherham, S60 1AS.	01709 363085
Dawson's Of Hillsborough, 70-72 Holme Lane, Sheffield, S6 4JW.	0114 2812178
Decathlon, Eyre St, Sheffield, S1 4QZ.	0114 2298190
Doncaster Angling Centre, 207 Carr House Rd, Doncaster.	01302 363629
First For Fishing, 148 Marshland Rd, Moorends, Doncaster.	01405 818277
Firth Park Angling, 7 Stubbin La, Sheffield, S5 6QG.	0114 2438631
Fishing Republic, Snape Hill Rd, Darfield, Barnsley, S73 9JU.	01226 752300
Francos Angling Supply, 148 High St, Bentley, Doncaster, DN5 0AT.	01302 874888
Goldthorpe Angling Centre, 53 High St, Rotherham S63 9LQ.	01709 893489
Gunnies Tackle, 297 Buchanan Rd, Sheffield, S5 8AU.	0114 2321437
G & S Hamstead, 14 Guardian Centre, Rotherham S65 1DD.	01709 365454
Handsworth Angling Centre, 7 Hendon St, Sheffield, S13 9AX.	0114 2696065
High Green Angling Centre, 1 Wortley Rd, Sheffield S35 4LQ.	0114 2845176
Ian's Fishing Tackle Shop, 303 Prince Of Wales Rd, Sheffield.	0114 2531533
Kerfoot's Fishing Tackle, 6 Southey Green Rd, Sheffield, S5 8GW.	0114 2313265
Killamarsh Angling Supplies, 120 Sheffield Rd, Killamarsh, S21 1EB	0114 2514936
Medusa, Unit 45 Princess Drive, Thurnscoe, Rotherham S63 0BL.	01709 582902
Mosborough Tackle Box, 38b High St, Sheffield, S19 5AE.	0114 2510664
Oakleys, 161-163 Northfield Rd, Sheffield, S10 1QQ.	0114 2681723
Parkgate Angling Centre, 19 Broad St, Parkgate, Rotherham, S62 6DX.	01709 527297
Pauls Fishing Tackle Centre, Doncaster Rd, Doncaster DN12 4HU.	01709 862558
Peg 31, Laughton Rd, Dinnington, Sheffield, S25 2PT.	01909 562552
R & R Sports, 40 High St, Bawtry, Doncaster, DN10 6JE.	01302 711130
Pete's Fishing Tackle, 65 Main St, Mexborough, S64 9ND.	01709 581715
Scawthorpe Fishing, 13 Crossland Way, Doncaster, DN5 9EX.	01302 789977
Six A.M Tackle + Bait, 82 Worksop Rd, Swallownest, Sheffield.	0114 2873070
Slippery Suckers, 30 Queens Drive, Barnsley, S72 8PB.	01226 711512
Snap & Tackle, 14 King Avenue, Doncaster DN11 0PG.	01302 863832
Stainforth Angling Ctr, 24 Silver St, Stainforth, Doncaster DN7 5AH.	01302 846623
Supabait, Common Lane, Clifton, Doncaster, DN12 2AL.	01709 863341
Swale Angling Centre, 738 Attercliffe Rd, Sheffield, S9 3RQ.	0114 2442398
Tackle Box, 7 Doncaster Rd, Barnsley, S70 1TH.	01226 247131
Tardis Tackle Angling Centre, 4 Sicey Ave, Sheffield.	0114 2436655
Thorne Pet & Angling, 5 The Green, Thorne, Doncaster, DN8 5AP.	01405 814056
Tight Lines Tackle, Glenshiel, Birley Moor Rd, Sheffield S12 4WG.	0114 2658178
Tigra Fishing Tackle, 14-15 Shopping Centre, Bellows Rd, Rawmarsh	01709 719252
Tony's Tackle, 10 Lidget Lane, Thurnscoe, Rotherham S63 0BU.	01709 880065
Universal Angling Supplies, 27a Mansfield Rd, Sheffield S12 2AE.	0114 2649664
Wickersley Angling Ctr, 2-4 Hellaby Ind Est, Rotherham, S66 8HR	01709 540998
Wombwell Angling Ctr, 25 Barnsley Rd, Barnsley S73 8HT.	01226 750659
Woodlands Angling, 232 Great North Rd, Doncaster, DN6 7HR	01302 728876
Woodseats Angling 625 Chesterfield Rd, Sheffield S8 0RX.	0114 2585133

I N D E X

	page no.
Abbeydale Dam	10
Aston Ponds	11
Bank End Fisheries	64
Barlow Coarse Fishery	12
Bradley Ponds	13
Bolton Brickponds	44
Candy Corner Fisheries	65
Carterhall Fishery	14
Crooks Valley Park	15
Crumwell Lane Pond	45
Dam Flask Reservoir	16
Dearne Valley Park Lake	46
Elmtree Farm Fisheries	47
Elsecar Reservoir	17
Ferryboat Farm Fisheries	48
Fleets Dam	49
Forge Dam	18
Grange Farm Lake	50
Graves Park Pond	19
Harlesthorpe Dam	66
Harthill Fisheries	67
Hatfield Water Park	68
Hayfield Fishing Lakes	69
Hillsborough Park Lake	20
Horseshoe Lake Coarse Fishery	70
Howbrook Dam	21
Kiveton Farm Fisheries	71
Kiverton Waters	72
KJS Aston Ponds	22
KJS Fisheries (Killamarsh)	23
Lewden Spring Fishery	24
Lindholme Lakes	73
Lodge Farm Fisheries	74
Long Pond, Barnaby Dun	51
Lowfield lakes	52
Loxley Fisheries	25
Milton Ponds	26
More Hall Water Gardens	27
Nancy Pond	28
Nether Mill Coarse Fishery	29
New Junction Canal	53
Newbiggin Pond	30
Norwood Cottage Farm Fisheries	31
Pebley Reservoir	75
Pinch Mill Fisheries	32
Plumpton Pond	54
Rivelin Dam	33
River Dearne	84
River Don	85
River Idle	87
River Rother	88
River Torne	89
Riverside Fisheries	76
Rother Valley Country Park	34
Roundwood Ponds	35
Sally Walsh's Dam	55
Smithies Reservoir	56
South Yorkshire Navigation canal	57
Straight Mile Fisheries	77
Stubbs Hall Lakes	58
Thorne Delves Fish Ponds	78
Tinkers Pond	59
Triangs Fishery	79
Tyram Hall Fisheries	80
Underbank Reservoir	36
Westwood Reservoir	37
West End Fisheries	38
Willow Garth	60
Wire Mill Dam Fishery	39
Wombwell Dam	61
Woodhouse Grange	81
Woodland Farm Fisheries	82
Worsbrough Canal	40
Worsbrough Reservoir	41

THIS VOUCHER CAN ONLY BE USED ONCE

HALF PRICE
DAY TICKET VOUCHER
Mon-Fri excluding bank holidays
Redeemable against ONE full adult day ticket price only
THIS VOUCHER IS INVALID IF REMOVED FROM BOOK

Signed by
LEWDEN SPRING BAILIFF

VALID UNTIL 31-10-08

THIS VOUCHER CAN ONLY BE USED ONCE

HALF PRICE
DAY TICKET VOUCHER
Mon-Fri excluding bank holidays
Redeemable against ONE full adult day ticket price only
THIS VOUCHER IS INVALID IF REMOVED FROM BOOK

Signed by
NETHER MILL COARSE FISHERY

VALID UNTIL 31-10-08

THIS VOUCHER CAN ONLY BE USED ONCE

HALF PRICE
DAY TICKET VOUCHER
FOR ONE PERSON AT ANY TIME
Redeemable against ONE full adult day ticket price only
THIS VOUCHER IS INVALID IF REMOVED FROM BOOK

Signed by
MILTON PONDS BAILIFF

VALID UNTIL 31-10-08

THIS VOUCHER CAN ONLY BE USED ONCE

FREE FISHING
DAY TICKET VOUCHER
ALLOWS ONE PERSON A DAYS FISHING FREE OF CHARGE
Mon-Fri excluding bank holidays
THIS VOUCHER IS INVALID IF REMOVED FROM BOOK

Signed by
NEWBIGGIN POND BAILIFF

VALID UNTIL 31-10-08

THIS VOUCHER CAN ONLY BE USED ONCE

FREE FISHING
DAY TICKET VOUCHER
ALLOWS ONE PERSON A DAYS FISHING FREE OF CHARGE
AT ANY TIME
THIS VOUCHER IS INVALID IF REMOVED FROM BOOK

Signed by
WESTWOOD RESERVOIR BAILIFF

VALID UNTIL 31-10-08

THIS VOUCHER CAN ONLY BE USED ONCE

£1.00 OFF
DAY TICKET VOUCHER
Mon or Fri excluding bank holidays
Redeemable against ONE full adult day ticket price only
THIS VOUCHER IS INVALID IF REMOVED FROM BOOK

Signed by
ROUNDWOOD PONDS BAILIFF

VALID UNTIL 30-6-07

THIS VOUCHER CAN ONLY BE USED ONCE

HALF PRICE
DAY TICKET VOUCHER
Mon-Fri excluding bank holidays
Redeemable against ONE full adult day ticket price only
THIS VOUCHER IS INVALID IF REMOVED FROM BOOK

Signed by
PINCH MILL BAILIFF

VALID UNTIL 31-10-08

THIS VOUCHER CAN ONLY BE USED ONCE

2 FOR 1
DAY TICKET VOUCHER
Mon-Fri excluding bank holidays
2 anglers fish for the price of a full adult day ticket
THIS VOUCHER IS INVALID IF REMOVED FROM BOOK

Signed by
MORE HALL BAILIFF

VALID UNTIL 31-10-08

THIS VOUCHER CAN ONLY BE USED ONCE

FREE FISHING
DAY TICKET VOUCHER
ALLOWS ONE PERSON A DAYS FISHING FREE OF CHARGE
AT ANY TIME
THIS VOUCHER IS INVALID IF REMOVED FROM BOOK

Signed by
ASTON PONDS BAILIFF

VALID UNTIL 31-10-08

THIS VOUCHER CAN ONLY BE USED ONCE

FREE HOT DRINK
+ HALF PRICE BAG OF PELLETS
Mon-Fri excluding bank holidays
THIS OFFER APPLIES TO ONE FULL PAYING ADULT DAY TICKET ANGLER ONLY
THIS VOUCHER IS INVALID IF REMOVED FROM BOOK

Signed by
LOXLEY FISHERIES BAILIFF

VALID UNTIL 31-10-08

THIS VOUCHER CAN ONLY BE USED ONCE

HALF PRICE
DAY TICKET VOUCHER
Mon-Fri excluding bank holidays
Redeemable against ONE full adult day ticket price only
THIS VOUCHER IS INVALID IF REMOVED FROM BOOK

Signed by
WIRE MILL DAM BAILIFF

WIRE MILL

VALID UNTIL 31-10-08

THIS VOUCHER CAN ONLY BE USED ONCE

HALF PRICE
DAY TICKET VOUCHER
Mon-Fri excluding bank holidays
Redeemable against ONE full adult day ticket price only
THIS VOUCHER IS INVALID IF REMOVED FROM BOOK

Signed by
NORWOOD FISHERIES BAILIFF

NORWOOD

VALID UNTIL 31-10-08

THIS VOUCHER CAN ONLY BE USED ONCE

HALF PRICE
DAY TICKET VOUCHER
Mon-Fri excluding bank holidays
Redeemable against ONE full adult day ticket price only
THIS VOUCHER IS INVALID IF REMOVED FROM BOOK

Signed by
LOWFIELD LAKES BAILIFF

LOWFIELD

VALID UNTIL 31-10-08

THIS VOUCHER CAN ONLY BE USED ONCE

FREE FISHING
DAY TICKET VOUCHER
ALLOWS ONE PERSON A DAYS COARSE FISHING FREE OF CHARGE
Mon-Fri excluding bank holidays
THIS VOUCHER IS INVALID IF REMOVED FROM BOOK

Signed by
BARLOW COARSE FISHERY

BARLOW

VALID UNTIL 31-10-08

THIS VOUCHER CAN ONLY BE USED ONCE

HALF PRICE
DAY TICKET VOUCHER
Mon-Fri excluding bank holidays
Redeemable against ONE full adult day ticket price only
THIS VOUCHER IS INVALID IF REMOVED FROM BOOK

Signed by
WILLOW GARTH PONDS BAILIFF

WILLOW GARTH

VALID UNTIL 31-10-08

THIS VOUCHER CAN ONLY BE USED ONCE

£1.00 OFF
DAY TICKET VOUCHER
AT ANY TIME
Redeemable against ONE full adult day ticket price only
THIS VOUCHER IS INVALID IF REMOVED FROM BOOK

Signed by
KJS FISHERIES (KILLAMARSH) BAILIFF

KJS FISHERIES

VALID UNTIL 31-10-08

THIS VOUCHER CAN ONLY BE USED ONCE

£1.00 OFF
DAY TICKET VOUCHER
AT ANY TIME
Redeemable against ONE full adult day ticket price only
THIS VOUCHER IS INVALID IF REMOVED FROM BOOK

Signed by
WEST END FISHERIES BAILIFF

WEST END

VALID UNTIL 31-10-08

THIS VOUCHER CAN ONLY BE USED ONCE

£2.00 OFF
DAY TICKET VOUCHER
Mon-Fri excluding bank holidays
Redeemable against ONE full adult day ticket price only
THIS VOUCHER IS INVALID IF REMOVED FROM BOOK

Signed by
FLEETS DAM BAILIFF

FLEETS DAM

VALID UNTIL 31-10-08

THIS VOUCHER CAN ONLY BE USED ONCE

£2.00 OFF
DAY TICKET VOUCHER
Mon-Fri excluding bank holidays
Redeemable against ONE full adult day ticket price only
THIS VOUCHER IS INVALID IF REMOVED FROM BOOK

Signed by
WOMBWELL DAM BAILIFF

WOMBWELL

VALID UNTIL 31-10-08

THIS VOUCHER CAN ONLY BE USED ONCE

HALF PRICE
DAY TICKET VOUCHER
Mon-Fri excluding bank holidays
Redeemable against ONE full adult day ticket price only
THIS VOUCHER IS INVALID IF REMOVED FROM BOOK

Signed by
FERRYBOAT FARM FISHERIES BAILIFF

FERRYBOAT

VALID UNTIL 31-10-08

THIS VOUCHER CAN ONLY BE USED ONCE

£2.00 OFF
DAY TICKET VOUCHER
Mon-Fri excluding bank holidays
Redeemable against ONE full adult day ticket price only
THIS VOUCHER IS INVALID IF REMOVED FROM BOOK

Signed by
KIVERTON FARM FISHERIES BAILIFF

VALID UNTIL 31-10-08

THIS VOUCHER CAN ONLY BE USED ONCE

£2.00 OFF
DAY TICKET VOUCHER
Mon-Fri excluding bank holidays
Redeemable against ONE full adult day ticket price only
THIS VOUCHER IS INVALID IF REMOVED FROM BOOK

Signed by
PEBLEY RESERVOIR BAILIFF

VALID UNTIL 31-10-08

THIS VOUCHER CAN ONLY BE USED ONCE

FREE FISHING
DAY TICKET VOUCHER
ALLOWS ONE PERSON A DAYS FISHING FREE OF CHARGE
AT ANY TIME
THIS VOUCHER IS INVALID IF REMOVED FROM BOOK

Signed by
WOODLAND FARM FISHERIES BAILIFF

VALID UNTIL 31-10-08

THIS VOUCHER CAN ONLY BE USED ONCE

HALF PRICE
DAY TICKET VOUCHER
Mon-Fri excluding bank holidays
Redeemable against ONE full adult day ticket price only
THIS VOUCHER IS INVALID IF REMOVED FROM BOOK

Signed by
WOODSEATS ANGLING SHOP FOR
ABBEYDALE DAM

VALID UNTIL 31-10-08

THIS VOUCHER CAN ONLY BE USED ONCE

HALF PRICE
DAY TICKET VOUCHER
Mon-Fri excluding bank holidays
Redeemable against ONE full adult day ticket price only
THIS VOUCHER IS INVALID IF REMOVED FROM BOOK

Signed by
TYRAM HALL FISHERY BAILIFF

VALID UNTIL 31-10-08

THIS VOUCHER CAN ONLY BE USED ONCE

£1.00 OFF
WEEKEND DAY TICKET
Weekend only
Redeemable against ONE full adult day ticket price only
THIS VOUCHER IS INVALID IF REMOVED FROM BOOK

Signed by
HARLESTHORPE DAM BAILIFF

VALID UNTIL 31-10-08

THIS VOUCHER CAN ONLY BE USED ONCE

£1.00 OFF
DAY TICKET VOUCHER
AT ANY TIME
Redeemable against ONE full adult day ticket price only
THIS VOUCHER IS INVALID IF REMOVED FROM BOOK

Signed by
KJS ASTON PONDS BAILIFF

VALID UNTIL 31-10-08

THIS VOUCHER CAN ONLY BE USED ONCE

FREE FISHING
DAY TICKET VOUCHER
ALLOWS ONE PERSON A DAYS FISHING FREE OF CHARGE
Mon-Fri excluding bank holidays
THIS VOUCHER IS INVALID IF REMOVED FROM BOOK

Signed by
NANCY POND BAILIFF

VALID UNTIL 31-10-08

THIS VOUCHER CAN ONLY BE USED ONCE

£1.00 OFF
DAY TICKET VOUCHER
Mon-Fri excluding bank holidays
Redeemable against ONE full adult day ticket price only
THIS VOUCHER IS INVALID IF REMOVED FROM BOOK

Signed by
RIVERSIDE FISHERY BAILIFF

VALID UNTIL 31-10-08

THIS VOUCHER CAN ONLY BE USED ONCE

HALF PRICE
DAY TICKET VOUCHER
Mon-Fri excluding bank holidays
Redeemable against ONE full adult day ticket price only
THIS VOUCHER IS INVALID IF REMOVED FROM BOOK

Signed by
CARTER HALL FISHERY BAILIFF

VALID UNTIL 31-10-08

New Fishery / Fishery Update Form

| Fishery Name | New Fishery ☐ |
| Update to Fishery ☐ |

Fishery Address

Post code

Contact Name

Telephone / Fax

| Adult Day Ticket Price | £ | concession OAP'S | £ |

Fish Species and Weights

Brief Description

Please e-mail or post a colour photo for inclusion in the next publication.

Please return this form to:
Arc Publishing and Print
166 Knowle Lane
Sheffield S11 9SJ